COLLECT

Other How To Books on business and management

Arranging Insurance
Be a Freelance Sales Agent
Buy & Run a Shop
Buy & Run a Small Hotel
Cash from Your Computer
Communicate at Work
Conduct Staff Appraisals
Conducting Effective Interviews
Conducting Effective Negotiations
Dealing with Your Bank
Doing Business Abroad
Do Your Own Advertising
Do Your Own PR
Employ & Manage Staff
Investing in People
Investing in Stocks & Shares
Keep Business Accounts
Manage a Sales Team
Manage an Office
Manage Computers at Work
Manage People at Work
Managing Budgets & Cash Flows
Managing Credit

Managing Meetings
Managing Yourself
Market Yourself
Master Book-Keeping
Master Public Speaking
Mastering Business English
Organising Effective Training
Prepare a Business Plan
Publish a Book
Publish a Newsletter
Raise Business Finance
Sell Your Business
Start a Business from Home
Start Your Own Business
Starting to Manage
Successful Mail Order Marketing
Taking on Staff
Understand Finance at Work
Use the Internet
Winning Presentations
Write a Report
Write & Sell Computer Software
Writing Business Letters

Further titles in preparation

The How To series now contains more than 200 titles in the following categories:

Business Basics
Family Reference
Jobs & Careers
Living & Working Abroad
Student Handbooks
Successful Writing

Please send for a free copy of the latest catalogue for full details (see back cover for address).

BUSINESS BASICS

COLLECTING A DEBT

How to enforce payment of
money owed to you

Roy Hedges

How To Books

Cartoons by Mike Flanagan

British Library Cataloguing in Publication Data
A catalogue record for this book is available from the British Library.

© Copyright 1997 by Roy Hedges.

First published in 1997 by How To Books Ltd, 3 Newtec Place,
Magdalen Road, Oxford OX4 1RE, United Kingdom.
Tel: (01865) 793806. Fax: (01865) 248780.

Note: The material contained in this book is set out in good faith for
general guidance and no liability can be accepted for loss or expense
incurred as a result of relying in particular circumstances on statements
made in the book. The laws and regulations are complex and liable to
change, and readers should check the current position with the relevant
authorities before making personal arrangements.

Produced for How To Books by Deer Park Productions.
Typeset by PDQ Typesetting, Stoke-on-Trent, Staffs.
Printed and bound by Cromwell Press, Broughton Gifford, Melksham,
Wiltshire.

Contents

List of illustrations

Preface

Running a business is difficult enough without the extra burden of customers keeping you waiting for the money they owe you. This is particularly true for the owners of smaller businesses, who are expected to manage the sales, marketing and stock control. Manufacturers have the added complication of production, quality control and delivery. You don't need the additional worry of cash flow, do you? If you recognise yourself in this scenario, then this book is for you. It is designed to help you overcome the problem of delinquent payers, and get what is owed to you into your bank account, so you can profitably maintain and expand your business. The opening chapters look at other ways of improving and protecting your cash flow – for example, credit insurance, invoice factoring and discounting.

However, unless you have been trained in or worked alongside the legal profession, the thought of going to court can be daunting. It doesn't matter if you as an individual have a grievance with a manufacturer over a product warranty, or are seeking compensation for poor holiday accommodation from a travel firm. You tend to shy away from pursuing a remedy via civil action. Perhaps you are a small businessman plagued with late paying customers – well, you can now bring effective action against your tardy payers without needing legal representation.

While the examples used throughout this book relate mainly to trade debts, the methods used are easily adaptable by an individual to settle most disputes not related to debt recovery. However, this does exclude divorce issues and arguments concerning care or conduct of children. So don't be put off by thinking this publication is for business use only. Whilst the majority of the text refers to civil actions in England, Wales and Northern Ireland, account of the variances relating to Scottish civil law has been clearly indicated in a chapter devoted to this subject.

Pride usually prevents most of us owning up to financial

difficulties; it is legal action which can overcome that pride in your customers. If your debtors bury their heads in the sand in the hope that you will not chase too hard, they are in for a shock. An important point to remember is, if an account remains unpaid for 70 days or more you could be making a loss on that sale. No business can afford to trade on these terms.

On the other hand some people delay paying their bills as long as possible. In business it is sometimes looked upon as a type of interest free overdraft. No more – this book explains dodges solicitors use to enforce judgement that they'll never tell you about, providing you with another valuable collection tool to add to your armoury. Use it wisely, and enjoy the benefits of improved cash flow to your business.

Finally, I wish to thank the following organisations for their assistance whilst researching this book. Without this help parts of the earlier chapters would not have been written:

> Commercial Collection Services
> Dun & Bradstreet
> Trade Indemnity Collections Ltd

Crown copyright is reproduced with the permission of the Controller of HMSO.

Roy A Hedges

IS THIS YOU?

Someone with a complaint or unsettled dispute

Credit controller · Accountant

Newsagent

Interpreter · Copy writer

Garage owner

Builder · Locksmith

Office equipment supplier

Surveyor · Hotelier

Importer

Shop fitter · Advertising agent

Office cleaner

Architect · Scaffolding contractor

Catering equipment supplier

Technical writer · Export agent

Draughtsman

Kennel owner · Art restorer

Gardener

Clothing manufacturer · Printer

Interior decorator

Designer · Carpenter

Stationer

Wholesaler · Marketing consultant

Metal finisher

Commercial artist · Glazier

Freight forwarder

Quantity surveyor · Plant hire contractor

Computer supplier

Property manager · French polisher

Carpet layer

Industrial dry cleaner · Express carrier

Builders merchant

Engraver · Galvaniser

Ships chandler

Dental technician · Model maker

Lithographic plate maker

Glass fibre moulder · Sign writer

Theatrical supplier

Marine engineer · Bookbinder

Safety equipment supplier · General manufacturer

1
Preparing Your Case

SOLVING DISPUTES
It is always advisable to avoid court action and settle your differences, or collect your debts amicably by negotiation. Issuing or threatening to issue a summons can sometimes do more harm than good. Litigation should be regarded as an action of last resort, especially in private disputes. This section is useful for disputes involving, for example:

- noisy neighbours
- boundary disputes
- complaints about faulty goods
- troublesome pets.

Deciding what you want
Making up your mind how you want to solve a particular dispute, before approaching the other party involved, is helpful in getting the result you want, whether it is:

- an apology
- someone to do or stop doing something
- compensation
- to be proved right
- money due to you.

Once you know the type of outcome you deserve, you can determine the best method to use to reach your goal.

Options available to you
You can deal with a person or organisation either directly or through a third party. But whichever method you use it should:

- get to the truth
- provide a remedy

- preserve a business relationship
- save your reputation.

Third party negotiation, including ombudsmen, court and non-court arbitration, is dealt with in Chapter 6.

Negotiating directly
This is the quickest and cheapest method of getting positive results. Unfortunately there can be problems with using this method, such as:

- you are too close to the person with whom you have a dispute
- if dealing with a company, you could be talking to a member of staff with whom you have a complaint.

What you must do
In direct negotiation, if you are unsure of your aims or not certain that your complaint is legitimate, to blunder ahead can simply make matters worse. Before contacting the party you are in dispute with, talk over your problem with a knowledgeable friend or go along to your nearest Citizens Advice Bureau. Now you can approach the other party with confidence, either by letter or face to face.

Speaking face to face
By far the best approach is face to face. After you have reached an agreement then you confirm it in writing. Don't just turn up on their doorstep, arrange the right time to talk. Always telephone for an appointment: it will get you nowhere if you arrive when the other party has just sat down to a meal. Nothing works better than if you arrive with a friendly smile. Before you go along to meet the other party be prepared, know exactly what you wish to say. Be clear in your mind what you want:

- know what the problem is
- how it affects you
- what you want them to do.

To make sure you do not overlook any important issues, list all of the points you want to get across.

Looking for common ground
Even agreeing to differ is a good beginning. Bring all issues into the open, and if you have more than one problem, solve the easy ones first. You must:

- be calm, friendly and put your problem over in a nice way
- listen to what the other side has to say
- don't get personal, separate the problem from the person
- look at all options before picking the best solution for you both.

It is advisable to keep notes of what is said and agreed.

Things you must avoid
Do not agree to any solution you consider unfair, or just for a quiet life. Never discuss any items not relating directly to the problem in hand. Above all you must not:

- interrupt, be abusive or lose your temper
- assume the other party knows the problem
- argue about what they have done
- assume others have the same values you do.

By letter
If you decide to settle your dispute by letter, set out the problem clearly and list the areas you are not happy with. After this tell the other side what you would like to see happen. Remember to keep copies of all correspondence between you both.

When negotiation fails
If all efforts to settle your disputes, or get the money due to you, by negotiation have been exhausted you are left with no choice but to seek a remedy through the legal system.

ANYONE CAN ISSUE A SUMMONS

It does not matter where you live or work in the British Isles, you can commence legal action in your nearest county, small claims or sheriff court. There are of course slight variations to the rules and procedures in different regions, and these changes are explained in the following chapters.

How the regions are defined
Briefly, the differing areas which mainly concern the reader split the British Isles into three. Each region has its own central office, known

Accounts Department,
Knavish & Co,
New Town Street,
Any Town,
County XZ1 1XZ.

19 July 199X

Dear Sirs,

TAKE NOTICE

Further to our earlier correspondence which you continue to ignore, your account remains unpaid, despite your unfulfilled promises of payment.

Having failed to settle the account for which a statement is itemised below, you are now informed that, unless payment of this account is received in full at these offices on or before the 18th day of November 199X, an application will be made at the Any Town County Court for leave to issue an ordinary summons against you for recovery of the understated amounts in full plus costs.

No further warning will be given.

ACCOUNT NUMBER: 001002ZXY.

Invoices delivered.   £

                                             £
                                   _____

                                   _____

Dated this .... day of .... 199...........

Signed: .... POSITION ....

Fig. 1. Example of a final notice letter.

as the Court Service. Primarily this office assists the local court staff and judges. It will accept enquiries from the general public, although your first port of call should always be your local county court.

England and Wales

In reality, there is now no limit to the value of a claim in the county court (the limit was £5,000). Changes to the county and small claims court rules in January 1996, increasing the limits in the small claims court from £1,000 to £3,000 when coupled with the facility to claim interest, gave access to redressing civil disputes in litigation to an increased number of people. Following the easy to understand guidelines in this book will give you the confidence to issue a summons, obtain and enforce judgement, without using a solicitor. Each chapter will guide you through preparing your case, giving evidence, and arguing against a defence.

Northern Ireland

The main differences in the lower courts of Northern Ireland are that the small claims limit is restricted to £1,000, and instead of issuing a summons you make an 'Application for arbitration'. If the respondent admits your claim he will advise the court by using an 'Acceptance of liability' form; if they do not reply the case is treated as undefended. To complete the forms, which are similar to those used in England and Wales, just follow the instructions given throughout this book. Other procedures and results remain unaffected.

Scotland

In Scotland actions for small claims are restricted to £750. The courts, procedures and the titles of their court officials are different from those in the rest of the British Isles. Chapter 11 has been devoted to these differences. So it does not matter where you or your debtors live and conduct business, this provides a comprehensive guide to settling your disputes and recovering the money owed to you.

SENDING A FINAL WARNING

Before going along to your local county court to issue a summons against a person or firm owing you money, it is advisable to send your debtor a letter warning of your intentions. Figure 1 gives you an idea of the format a final notice should take, together with the information you should include to allow your debtor an opportunity to settle the outstanding debt. Nevertheless, you are leaving your wayward customer in no doubt of your intentions should the warning be ignored by them, including the extra costs that will be added to the outstanding account.

Waiting for your debtor to pay
It is usually lack of income which has caused the debt to accrue in the first place. In this case the debtor will often wish to avoid the embarrassment of a county court judgement being registered against them, which will affect their future credit applications. They may, therefore, offer to pay the amount by weekly or monthly instalments. If this does happen, you must consider very carefully the amount offered and the time it will take to recover the debt. You must then weigh this against the cost of going to court – which may only result in judgement being granted for a similar or lower amount.

Accepting payment by instalments
If you accept payment of the debt at set regular intervals, it is important to confirm the arrangements in writing. Always enclose an extra copy of the letter for your debtor to sign and return to you. This will resolve any doubts should future action be necessary. The letter must clearly state:

● the total overall period the arrangement will take to complete

● the frequency and amount of each payment required to settle the matter in the agreed timescale

● the percentage rate and amount of interested agreed, if applicable.

The letter confirming all the above details **must always** include the following paragraph:

'If any one of the agreed instalments is not paid on the date stipulated, the balance of the outstanding debt becomes due and payable.'

Significance of this paragraph
If an instalment is not paid or a cheque bounces, you may sue only for the missing payment if this clause is excluded from your letter. You will then be faced with issuing a series of costly and time wasting summonses for each unpaid instalment. Your only other alternative is to wait for the date of the final payment to lapse. Then, and only then, could you sue for the whole of the outstanding balance.

A sample letter confirming an arrangement to pay by instalments, incorporating this important paragraph, is shown in Figure 2. Now, if your customer misses one single payment, the balance of the outstanding account can be claimed.

Writing a final demand letter

Your name, address and telephone number should be clearly stated on the final demand. If you are a businessman, your letterhead will suffice. The date of the demand must be distinct and include sufficient information for your customer to identify the amount of their indebtedness, the period of time they have to discharge their liability, and naturally the destination of the payment. Further, it must state precisely the actions you will take if the demand is ignored. Once a final demand is sent and your debtor fails to pay, you must be prepared to follow through with your stated caution, in the final demand letter.

Showing cause for the demand
The debtor, by refusing to pay the amount owed and continually ignoring your requests for payment, gives ample cause. You are left with little or no option but to seek a legal remedy against their default.

Amount due to be paid
Clearly state the full amount owed by the debtor to yourself, including the date(s) on which the debt arose.

Reason why you are owed the amount claimed
It could be for goods ordered and delivered, services supplied or work done. Perhaps it is for rent or money lent. Whatever the explanation never leave your debtor in any doubt why the money is owed to you. Otherwise it may be used as an excuse for non-payment when they are in court.

Time and place of payment
Determine the time and place you require the amount claimed to be paid, to avoid continuance of your action. State these in a lucid and positive manner.

If the demand is ignored
Inform the debtor of your intentions, should they fail to comply with the final notice, by making known at which court you will issue the summons to enforce payment of the outstanding debt plus any additional costs.

E Knavish Esq,
Knavish & Co,
New Town Street,
Any Town,
County ZX1 1XZ.   28 July 199X

Dear Mr Knavish

Re: ACCOUNT NO: 001002XYZ.   BALANCE: £2,432.16p.

I refer to your recent offer to pay the overdue balance of your
account, as stated above, by regular monthly payments.

In view of the circumstances explained, I am agreeable to you
discharging the sum outstanding over a six month period.

The total sum is therefore to be paid by five (5) equal
instalments of £400.00p. each. The first such instalment is to be
paid on the first day of September 199X. Then on the first day
of each and every subsequent month. The final payment of
£432.16p is to be paid on the first day of February 199X.

If any one of the agreed instalments is not paid on the date
stipulated, the balance of the outstanding debt becomes due
and payable forthwith.

It is further agreed that future orders will be accepted from you
during this period, subject to those orders not exceeding
£500.00p in any one month. Payments for these items are
strictly cash on delivery. This arrangement will be reviewed on
satisfactory settlement of the above debt.

Please confirm, your acceptance of the above agreement by
signing, dating and returning to this office the enclosed copy by
return of post.

Yours sincerely,

Bill Swift
PROPRIETOR

Fig. 2. Example of a letter agreeing to an offer to pay by instalments.

PREVENTING A DEFENCE

Avoiding costly mistakes at the outset is easier and certainly more cost effective than trying to remedy them at a later stage of your collection process, when perhaps the facts relating to an unpaid account are a little unclear.

Confirming your debt cannot be disputed

Check your records thoroughly before sending a final demand. Be certain you have a debt and it is overdue for payment. This will save you time and money, leaving you free to get on with your other business commitments. Most importantly, it can avoid you losing a valuable customer.

Have you been paid?
Make sure your customer has not paid what you say is still outstanding. They may have sent a cheque and it was posted to the wrong account. Perhaps when they sent their cheque they omitted to identify which account it was for, or you were unable to make out the sender, and it's sitting in your unallocated items account.

Check they received the goods or services ordered
Did your customer receive all the goods ordered? Did you complete the service call? Was part of the order damaged? Before you issue a summons ensure you have a clean provable debt – one your debtor will be unable to dispute.

Telephone your customer
Misunderstandings can be avoided if you speak to your customer. However, you must not accept any more excuses. If an unacceptable reason for non-payment is given, leave your customer in no doubt of your intentions if they fail to pay as requested. Remember, it can be profitable to talk.

- Try to discover the reason they have not paid.

- Confirm they are not waiting for an order to be completed.

- Are they expecting you to exchange damaged goods?

- Have you finished the work ordered to their satisfaction?

Keep a brief note of all the important items discussed during your telephone conversation with your customer. It may prove useful as additional evidence when attending the court hearing, although technically it is usually not allowable.

GETTING YOUR FACTS RIGHT

Reconciling the account
Confirm you have done your sums and the invoice totals are accurate. Make sure figures have not been transposed. For example, have you written £71 on your customer's sales ledger account when it should be £17? Also check if the prices on your invoice tally with the prices quoted, and the number of items charged on the invoice agree with those delivered and signed for on the delivery note.

Check again
Never give a customer's account a quick glance, check every item carefully. Make sure your customer does not have any outstanding complaints about your goods or service that you haven't dealt with.

Internal case preparation
These primary steps for preparing your case before issuing a summons are to ensure you have a clean provable debt: one which cannot be disputed in any form. This avoids costly and time consuming hearings and ensures you get the money owed to you in the shortest time possible.
   Therefore you must confirm:

• all goods and services have been provided

• your customer owes you what you say they do

• there are no outstanding complaints

• a final demand notice was sent.

You will find this information by:

• checking delivery and consignment notes

• reconciling your sales ledger

• checking your customer query files and questioning your staff

• telephoning your customer.

Advantages

There are important issues to learn when preparing your first case for litigation. Initially it will be a time consuming exercise. But if you ensure simple mistakes are avoided on a regular basis, subsequent preparations for legal action will take less time. Your business will benefit from the improved methods, becoming more efficient and profitable. Improved cash flow will be clearly evident. Failure to observe these basic business principles can lead to loss of customer loyalty, and in extreme situations loss of your business.

QUESTIONS AND ANSWERS

Why try to negotiate a settlement?

It is always advantageous to reach a conclusion both parties are happy with, rather than damaging friendships or long-standing business arrangements which would be difficult to replace.

Is sending a final demand a legal requirement?

No. You are not obliged to warn your customer that you are about to issue a summons against them.

So why send one?

It will assist when asking for judgement against your customer if you can assure the court you gave your customer every opportunity to settle the debt without resorting to legal action. There is also a chance your debtor will cough up and pay what they owe you.

Why telephone my customer if he's refused to pay in the past?

It confirms your records are correct. This last call enquiring about complaints removes all excuses for non-payment from your customer when he is in court. It will also reassure the court of your efforts to get an amicable settlement.

Isn't it up to the customer to prove he doesn't owe me money?

No. You have to satisfy the court the debt is due and payable. So careful preparation is vital to your case.

Why not wait until the hearing and let the customer argue?

If your case is prepared properly, your customer will be unable to submit a defence to your claim – possibly allowing you to obtain judgement by post, without having to attend court.

When should I sue?

Not until after the agreed credit period has expired. Credit is never allowed unless it has been previously agreed. The Sale of Goods Act 1979 Section 28 provides that 'delivery and payment are to be concurrent unless otherwise agreed'.

Do I need a solicitor?

No. By following the step-by-step procedures in this book, it is possible to issue a summons, obtain and enforce a judgement order without the aid of legal representation and formal legal training.

Will my case be affected if I do not use a solicitor?

Not at all. It is not a requirement in the lower courts that you must use a solicitor. In fact these courts are designed for small claims which are without legal representation. It is only in the High Court that you must be represented by a lawyer or solicitor and counsel.

Which court should I use: lower or higher?

In most cases it will be either the small claims or county courts. Only claims in excess or £25,000, or cases which may set a new precedent in law, are heard in the High Court. Chapter 3 deals with this question, so you have no need to worry.

CHECKLIST

Does your **final warning** contain:

- the reason the final demand is being sent

- amount claimed

- dates the debt arose

- details of goods or services supplied

- when and where to pay

- the outcome if the demand is ignored.

CASE STUDIES

Introduction

We shall now introduce three entirely fictional case study characters (any resemblance to living persons is unintended and completely coincidental). Two of our characters are plaintiffs suing for a debt; the third is a defendant. We will examine how the two plaintiffs prepare and issue a summons. At the same time we shall look at how a defendant could act and what he must do upon receiving a summons. Once judgement has been granted we shall examine the various methods of enforcement.

Bill Swift thinks only big business can sue

Bill Swift inherited the business from his father 15 years ago. He hires a range of goods and mechanical equipment to small businesses, self employed tradesmen and the general public. He offers trade customers 30 days' credit accounts. For the DIY enthusiast his hire terms are strictly COD. He chases overdue debts only by sending a series of reminder letters and hopes his customers will pay. After a time he writes off the debts of those who do not pay. Suing a customer is only what big businesses do, he thinks.

Karen Turner believes only solicitors can issue summons

Two years ago Karen turner joined a limited company as a credit controller and was recently promoted. Whilst she is good at her job, Karen lacks the confidence to issue a summons, believing this can only be done by qualified solicitors. Karen is also uncertain about the procedure to follow after judgement has been granted. She believes legal proceedings should be used as a last resort, when all other methods for collecting overdue debts have been exhausted.

Ted Knavish receives a summons

Ted Knavish was made redundant three years ago. Until then he had been employed for over ten years as a gardener with the local authority parks department. Together with his son, he set up as a landscape gardening contractor. To avoid tying up their limited capital in expensive equipment, they usually hire such things as cement mixers and mechanical diggers from Swift's hire shop. Ted's wife looks after the book-keeping. They try to avoid paying any outstanding accounts until they have been paid themselves. This sometimes annoys their suppliers. So when he receives a summons from Bill Swift, he is surprised and angry.

DISCUSSION POINTS

1. Do you always pay bills as or before they fall due?

2. Are your records good enough to prove that your debtor has had every opportunity to pay?

3. Should litigation be the last resort?

2
Identifying Your Debtor

WHOM DO I SUE?

This question may seem irrelevant; in fact it could be considered ridiculous. After all, you have been telephoning your customer and banging on their door long enough to know who to issue a summons against and where. If a customer has not settled their account within your specified trading terms and has continually ignored your requests for payment, it will be obvious whom you must sue, won't it? Not necessarily! Simply because you have dealt with a customer over a prolonged period of time, it does not mean you really know their true identity or trading structure.

Knowing your debtor
You have spoken to both Mr and Mrs Knavish and their son from time to time. So when they default and you issue a summons to recover the money owed to you, obviously it must be addressed to Mr Knavish of Knavish & Co. But although you have dealt with this firm for some time in this semblance, it may not be their correct trading or registered title. There will be times when speaking to a customer, you thought you were talking to the owner of the business. Unfortunately, it may only be a coincidence that the employee you have been speaking to all this time had the same name as your customer. Your demands for payment had been falling on deaf ears for a very long time. Perhaps this is why payment has sometimes been late, and now it has not been paid at all.

EXPLORING LEGAL ENTITIES

Getting the details of your customer right should be your number one priority. In fact your customer could be trading in any number of guises, such as:

- a sole trader

- a partnership
- a limited company.

Other entities you may come across could be:

- social clubs
- limited partnerships
- charities.

It is important that your summons is issued to the right party. If you have the wrong name or use a branch address instead of the head or registered office your case will be struck out, costing you money in unnecessary court fees and wasting your time re-issuing the summons. You will then have to wait again for the statutory time to elapse before applying for judgement and, most importantly, getting the money owed to you into your bank account and not your customer's. The primary source of information about your customer's trading style is of course their letterheading or cheques. Both of these can be very useful documents for basic knowledge of your debtor.

Taking precautions

Being unaware of the correct trading style and title of your customer and the extent of their liabilities is a primary cause of financial loss, resulting in many small business failures. Usually the euphoria of getting a new customer, especially in a small business, tends to make one careless. By ensuring a simple 'New Account Form' is completed by each new customer, setting out fundamental information, you will avoid needless errors and prevent bad debts from occurring. Remember, credit is not a right to be demanded by a customer. You should only grant it where you see fit, retaining the right to refuse or withdraw credit facilities at any time.

Avoiding confusion

It is advisable to display your terms of trade clearly on all documents. These should include invoices, despatch notes and monthly statements sent or given to your customer. In reality they should be printed clearly and define the period of credit allowed together with the payment arrangements you expect, leaving your customer in no doubt of your intentions should they be ignored.

Defining entities

An explanation of the differing types of entities, the extent of individual liabilities, against whom to address your action and the reasoning behind the decision are given below, demonstrating the variety of debtors there are and the importance of knowing who your customer really is.

Sole trader
The sole trader is, as the name implies, a person who sets up business in their own right. They may trade under their own name, or use a trading title. A landscape gardener could trade as 'Blooming Designs', for example. So if issuing a summons against a sole trader you will claim against Mr E Knavish or Mr E Knavish trading as 'Blooming Designs'. It will assist in identifying your debtor if you can state his first names. Once judgement is obtained against a sole trader and they fail to pay, you can levy distraint against not only the business assets but their personal ones as well.

A partnership
A partnership consists of two or more people getting together to trade as one. Accountants and solicitors are typical examples of partnerships. But any type of trade or profession can trade in this manner. So, when a partnership firm fails to pay their bills, all the individual partners are equally responsible for payment of your account. It does not matter if they were the ones who originated the debt or not.

In the case of a partnership, it is advisable to issue the summons against each individual partner at their home address and not against the partnership as a firm, at its trading address. If a judgement is granted and you have issued the summons against the partnership, only the trading assets of the partnership can be seized. On the other hand, if you had summoned each partner individually at their private residence, each and every one is liable to pay what is owed to you, giving you a much better chance of recovery.

A limited company
Your debtor might be trading as a company registered under the Companies Act, which means the company is a separate entity from its directors and managers. You can only sue the company in its own right. If a company fails to pay a judgement order you can only enforce payment against the company's assets, not against any of the directors – unless you were given a personal guarantee (with normal trade debts this is extremely rare).

Social clubs
When trading with a social club, which could include a golf club or a working men's club, it is advisable to check the rules and how they are managed. Knowing the responsibility of all the club's members is indispensable information when seeking a judgement order. Maybe only the club's secretary, treasurer or chairperson are responsible for paying the club's debts. In some instances the whole of the committee or perhaps the full membership of the club could be personally liable for the settlement of the debt to you.

Other trading entities
You may come across partnerships and companies which are limited by guarantee. These are usually non profit-making organisations, such as charities. There may be a few limited partnerships whose partners will have some form of protection similar to those enjoyed by a company director, but they are rare now.

Cutting out mistakes
Eliminating errors of identity and establishing levels of responsibility in your limited company customers are important to maintaining a profitable business. The use of a standard yet simple new customer account or credit form should become normal procedure, no matter what the size of your business.

The form must include the fullest details of:

- names and addresses of all directors or partners
- degrees of liability for sanctioning payment
- principal trading address or registered office
- relevant bank details
- the name of the person responsible for your account.

All information supplied must be verified.

Safeguarding your cash flow
Another method of identifying your customer, and at the same time safeguarding your cash flow, is to use the services of invoice factors or credit insurers. However, there are certain limitations imposed: for example, some will stipulate the minimum annual sales turnover you must have before they will consider you. This is usually around £350,000.

Taking out credit insurance
It is possible to insure your UK and overseas trade debts against insolvency and non-payment. Between 75 and 90 per cent of your sales invoice balance can be covered. The insurers will insist on checking the creditworthiness of all your customers, and give advice on credit risk. Services can be tailored to your own requirements, and you will find premiums can vary between insurers, so shop around. They will almost certainly exclude your riskier customers from the arrangement. Before rushing out and insuring your sales ledger debt, carefully weigh up the overall cost of insurance cover. It is certainly worth considering if you are an exporter, as their intelligence service relating to overseas markets is essential to any business.

Invoice factoring
Basically, this is another way to borrow money. To assist you with your cash flow an invoice discount or factoring company will advance cash against your sales invoices. They will in certain contracts also insist on managing your sales ledger, for a fee. Again the level of fees, interest charges and service varies among rival firms. They will not improve your collection performance.

If considering this method of improving your cash flow, make sure your customers are paying promptly, even if this means getting in a specialist consultant. In addition to the monthly fees, you will be charged interest on the money they pay to you. This will be levied from the time they receive your invoices for factoring until they receive payment from your customers. Usually the amount of advance you receive is between 70 to 80 per cent of your invoice value. The balance is paid to you less interest and charges at the end of the credit period allowed. The factor will check out your customers' credit rating, and will exclude the riskier elements from the arrangements. Normally invoice factoring or discounting falls into four main categories, these are:

Recourse:	This means if your customer does not pay or becomes insolvent, you must refund all the money advanced.
Non recourse:	With this type of agreement you will be insured against non-payment and the insolvency of your customer. Naturally higher fees are charged, and strict conditions can be laid down in respect of all or some of your customers' credit limits. The factor may also refuse this service for specific customers.

Disclosure: Your customers will be aware of your arrange-
                     ments with the factors. You will send out your
                     invoices in the normal manner, but each invoice
                     will bear a message telling your customer to pay
                     the factor. It's the factors who'll now send out
                     monthly statements and chase for payments.
Non disclosure: In this agreement you will handle all the in-
                     house sales ledger systems with the factor
                     monitoring them discreetly. Your customer
                     will be unaware that you are factoring your
                     sales invoices. This service is usually reserved
                     for the medium and larger size businesses.

It is true that factoring can provide a vital service to small
businesses, but generally speaking they will not improve your own
collection performance. The factor, like the credit insurer, will check
out all your customers and agree credit limits with you. What you
have to consider when using a factor is the loss of control of an
important asset, your sales ledger debt, and whether having an
additional source of finance is worth the extra costs involved.

CHECKING YOUR DEBTOR IS WORTH SUING

It is worth your while to confirm your debtor has the financial
means to satisfy any judgement you may obtain, before issuing a
summons. Neglecting this simple step will only add extra costs to
your existing losses. To establish if your customer is worth suing,
you can either:

- contact your trade association
- use a credit reference agency
- instruct a debt collector.

Contacting your trade association
Some business groups have trade associations, a sort of trade union
for business people. They meet periodically to exchange information, provide assistance and guidance where practicable, and
generally represent their members' interests in the press or by
lobbying parliament. If you are having difficulties with a particular
customer, why not discuss these with other members of your trade
association at their local meetings. They could also be experiencing
problems with the same customer, thus providing another excellent

source for information. Openly discussing delinquent payers with fellow members of a trade association in private does not contravene the Data Protection Act.

Using a credit reference agency

Using a credit reference agency is advisable when taking on a new credit customer. They are also a great help when deciding if your customer is worth suing by instructing them to undertake a pre-sue search. The fee charged for this service depends on the volume of information required. These fees can and do differ marginally from firm to firm. The length of time it takes to provide the information requested also varies depending on how busy the agency is at the time of contact. It is well worth enquiring about any time delay when instructing an agency. A list of details the credit reference agencies can supply are itemised in the section 'Doing a pre-sue search' below.

Instructing a debt collection agency

Some debt collecting agencies also provide credit references. It may be prudent to instruct a debt collector to recover your debt before considering issuing a summons. There are many debt collectors, each one operating differing methods. Broadly speaking there are two types when it comes to charges:

1. One uses a voucher system, which means for a fixed payment you purchase a number of vouchers, usually in book form. Every time a bad debt arises you fill in the details on the voucher, and send it to the agency, who will contact your debtor by sending a series of collection letters at regular intervals. Each letter is more strongly worded than the previous one. This service is fine for smaller debts, but it does mean you are paying in advance.

2. The second type charges on a no collection no fee basis. As you only pay if they are successful, they tend to be a little more vigorous in chasing for payment. But they will only chase as hard as you instruct them to. Once your debtor has paid, they charge you a percentage of the amount collected. As the percentage rate varies from collector to collector, it is advisable to telephone and enquire about their fees and services before issuing formal instructions. The larger collection agencies also operate a letter cycle system for smaller accounts.

If your debtor has gone away, most of the agencies operate a tracing service, for which an additional fee will be charged, if successful. Should your debtor be an individual they can also find out where he is working. The importance of this will be seen in Chapter 8 relating to enforcing judgement.

LEARNING OF YOUR DEBTORS' LIABILITIES

Doing a pre-sue search
This will contain as much or as little information as you require. The agency's fee will be charged according to the amount of information requested.

Basically the facts you require to know about your debtor are:

- any other judgements registered against them
- if they have sufficient income to pay you
- their correct trading title
- if a limited company, their registered office
- all charges against the business for debentures, secured loans and mortgages
- details of all bank accounts
- names and addresses of all partners
- date of last filed accounts
- list of assets.

Register of judgements
For a small fee you can search the register of county court judgements. If your customer has previous unsatisfied judgements registered against them, they will be listed. This service can be used at any time – when granting credit, for example. The register only gives details of county court judgements: it does not supply you with the information you get from a pre-sue search, which will also list outstanding judgements.

QUESTIONS AND ANSWERS

Is a sole trader's spouse also liable?

Only if she is a partner in the business, or has signed a guarantee indemnifying the debtor.

Why can't a director of a limited company be sued?

When a company is registered a separate legal entity is formed. Its cash and assets are completely separate from those of the directors and shareholders. When a limited company fails its shareholders' liabilities are limited to the amount they agreed to invest.

Are there any exceptions to this rule?

Yes. If the directors of a limited company allowed the company to trade whilst it was insolvent, or if the company traded with fraudulent intentions. Unfortunately, experience has shown these are difficult circumstances to prove.

Is a pre-sue search really necessary?

It saves you spending any further money on an uncollectable debt. In addition it provides vital information, which will help you decide the most effective method of enforcement when you have obtained a judgement order against your debtor.

How can I locate a credit reference agency?

Your local *Yellow Pages* is a good starting point. A couple of firms are listed in the Useful Addresses section at the end of this book.

How long will I have to wait for a pre-sue search?

If you use a credit agency on a regular basis, you can fax your instructions and in most cases have a reply on the same day. Otherwise, if you send a payment with your request, by return of post is usual; certainly you will not wait more than a couple of days.

CHECKLIST

- Do you know who to sue?
- Have you explored the differing entities?
- Is your customer worth suing?
- Have you undertaken a pre-sue search?
- List all the things you must do before issuing a summons.

CASE STUDIES

Bill gets fed up waiting

Tired of waiting for his accounts to be paid Bill Swift instructs a firm of debt collectors. They send Knavish & Co a letter, followed by another a week or so later, a little more forceful this time. (Some collection agencies would telephone Bill's customer, if this was in his instructions.) When all these methods have been exhausted they, or more probably Bill Swift, will send his customer a final demand letter. The larger debt collecting agencies can supply Bill Swift with a pre-sue search for an additional charge.

Karen contacts a credit reference agency

After contacting a credit reference agency, Karen Turner is impressed with the speed of their response and the information supplied about her company's debtor. Realising that most of this information should be known to her before allowing credit, Karen decides to use a new customer account form in future. With her larger customers she plans to undertake a credit check before granting credit from now on. Karen also proposes to review the account on a regular basis thereafter. Now Karen has details of her customer's assets and liabilities, she is aware they can afford to pay what is owed, and sends them a final notice.

Ted gets annoyed

Receiving letters from debt collectors and final demand notices from both Karen Turner and Bill Swift, Ted Knavish wonders what all the fuss is about. Turning to his wife, he shouts angrily 'What's up with these people, don't they know I will pay eventually? I have always paid in the past – perhaps a little late, but I've paid.' Without waiting for an answer he throws the final demands in the wastepaper bin, hoping Karen and Bill were bluffing.

DISCUSSION POINTS

1. Weigh the benefits of invoice factoring and credit insurance against their disadvantages.

2. What would be the importance to you of the pre-sue search?

3. Could you categorise your customers according to their legal entities?

3
Time to Sue

MAKING YOUR CLAIM

Having thoroughly completed all the preliminary work, and
contented yourself you have an undisputed claim and your debtor
has the means to satisfy your judgement in full if granted, it is now
time to go along to your local county court and collect form N1 to
issue your summons. Whilst at the court house ask for a current list
of court fees as reference will be made from time to time to including
court fees when issuing various actions. The actual sums cannot be
quoted, as these fees are liable to change.

Which court do I use?
Generally speaking there is not any choice about which court you
must use. This is governed by several aspects, over which you have
little control. Usually most claims and especially trade debts are
heard in the county or small claims court. Briefly the functions of
the differing courts are:

High court
To use the high court you must employ a solicitor. This will usually
lead to a barrister also being appointed. Now costs start to mount,
which you may have to pay partially or fully before action
commences. Of course the bulk of these fees will be recovered.
However, remember that not all the costs you will incur are
automatically granted against the defendant if you win.

To be heard in the high court your claim must satisfy one or more
of the following:

- it is setting a precedent in law
- it is in excess of £25,000
- the defendant has a high counterclaim
- the court feels it is in your or the defendant's interest for the case
  to be heard in a higher court.

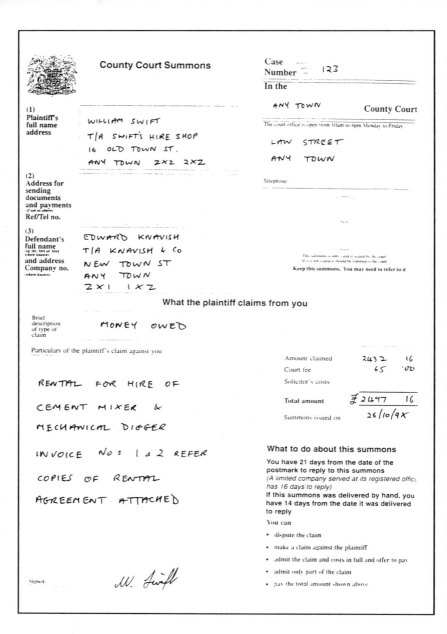

County Court Summons

Case Number: 123

In the ANY TOWN County Court

The court office is open from 10am to 4pm Monday to Friday

LAW STREET
ANY TOWN

Telephone:

This summons is only valid if sealed by the court
If it is not sealed it should be reported to the court
Keep this summons. You may need to refer to it

(1) Plaintiff's full name address

WILLIAM SWIFT
T/A SWIFT'S HIRE SHOP
16 OLD TOWN ST.
ANY TOWN 2X2 2X2

(2) Address for sending documents and payments (if not as above) Ref/Tel no.

(3) Defendant's full name (eg Mr, Mrs or Miss where known) **and address Company no.** (where known)

EDWARD KNAVISH
T/A KNAVISH & Co
NEW TOWN ST
ANY TOWN
2 X 1 1 X 2

What the plaintiff claims from you

Brief description of type of claim

MONEY OWED

Particulars of the plaintiff's claim against you

RENTAL FOR HIRE OF
CEMENT MIXER &
MECHANICAL DIGGER

INVOICE Nos 1 & 2 REFER

COPIES OF RENTAL
AGREEMENT ATTACHED

Amount claimed   2432   16
Court fee   65   00
Solicitor's costs

Total amount   £ 2497   16
Summons issued on   26/10/9X

What to do about this summons

You have 21 days from the date of the postmark to reply to this summons
(A limited company served at its registered office has 16 days to reply)
If this summons was delivered by hand, you have 14 days from the date it was delivered to reply

You can

- dispute the claim
- make a claim against the plaintiff
- admit the claim and costs in full and offer to pay
- admit only part of the claim
- pay the total amount shown above

Signed   W. Swift

Fig. 3. Sample form for issuing a summons (N1).
(This form is reproduced with permission of HMSO.)

County court

Most claims are heard either in the county or small claims court: particularly those relating to normal trade debts, and most private disputes. Using the county court is a simple matter, and depending on where you trade and the volume of business before the court, it can be quicker, and will certainly cost less, than using the high court, and it is just as effective. The positive aspects of using the county court against that of the high court are:

• there is less pomp and formality

• you can claim interest until amount is paid if claim is £5,000 and over or up to date of judgement on sums under £5,000

• you can issue a summons, get judgement and enforce payment without using a solicitor.

Small claims court

The only difference between the county and small claims court is the value of your claim. A small claim is one that is less than £3,000. You will issue a summons for a small claim in your local county court. Most small claims relate to unpaid bills, but may be for:

• bad workmanship
• faulty goods
• accidents
• damage to property
• goods not delivered.

ISSUING A SUMMONS

To issue a summons you must first complete three copies of form N1. One copy is for you, another for the court, and the third will be sent to the defendant. Write clearly to avoid errors and to ensure the document is remitted to the correct address. A completed sample of form N1 is shown in Figure 3.

Completing the forms

If you are suing partners of a firm, you will require a copy of form N1 for each individual partner. The following information will be required on this form:

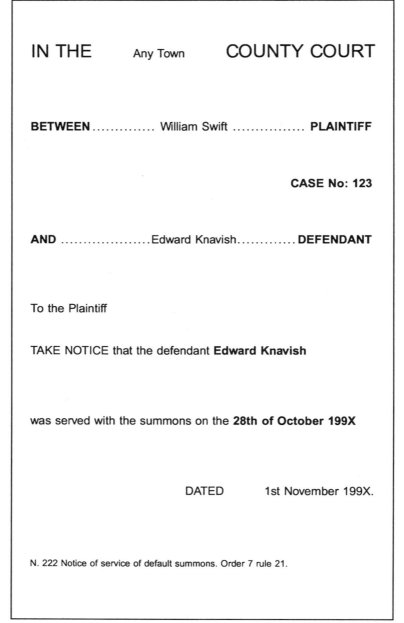

IN THE   Any Town   COUNTY COURT

BETWEEN .... William Swift .... **PLAINTIFF**

CASE No: 123

AND .... Edward Knavish .... **DEFENDANT**

To the Plaintiff

TAKE NOTICE that the defendant **Edward Knavish**

was served with the summons on the **28th of October 199X**

DATED   1st November 199X.

N. 222 Notice of service of default summons. Order 7 rule 21.

Fig. 4. Notice of service of summons (N222).
(Reproduced by permission of HMSO.) Note: Form N216 is similar in
structure to the above, except it will state the reason for non-service.

Box 1.   State your own or business name and address in full.
Box 2.   Your address for service. Complete the section only if you wish the court to send documents and payments to you at a different address.
Box 3.   Defendant's name and address. If a company their company number if known (the pre-sue search will supply this information).

Underneath these boxes details of your claim should be entered such as:

- brief description of your claim
- particulars of claim
- amount claimed plus the cost of the court fee.

WHAT MUST I DO NOW?

Take or send the completed forms along to your local county court. If you are submitting the forms by post a stamped, self addressed envelope should always be included. The court staff will use this to send you form N222. That is the 'Notice of Service', an example of which is shown in Figure 4. This notice will quote a 'case' or 'plaint number': this is your reference number, and must be cited each time you contact the court. This form also acts as your receipt for the fees paid.

What happens at the court

The court staff will post a copy of the summons together with reply forms N9A and B to the defendant. On the reverse side of the summons are notes informing the defendants what they must do, and the length of time they have to reply. Service of a summons is always by first class post, unless you wish it to be served by a bailiff (an additional fee is charged for bailiff service, and paid at the time of issue). Within 14 days from the date of service the defendant must do one of four things:

1. Pay the full amount claimed.
2. Admit they owe the money and make an offer to pay.
3. Submit a defence.
4. Ignore the summons.

Both of the above forms will be dealt with in Chapters 4 and 5. It is advisable to make a diary note on the 15th day after the summons was served, to make enquiries at the court and check what action

Notice of Application

Plaintiff / ~~defendant's~~ address

16, OLD TOWN ST.

ANY TOWN

Z×Z Z×Z

In the ANY TOWN	County Court
Case no. 123	
Warrant no.	
Plaintiff WILLIAM SWIFT	
Defendant EDWARD KNAVISH	

I wish to apply for

REISSUE OF SUMMONS

THE PLAINTIFF STILL RESIDES AT THE
ADDRESS STATED ON FORM N1

MR KNAVISH IS 5'11" TALL, DARK HAIRED.
HE HAS A TATTOO OF A FLOWER ON HIS
RIGHT FOREARM WITH THE NAME HAY
UNDERNEATH

Signed _M. Swift_ .... Plaintiff / ~~Defendant~~ Dated 14/11/9x

Address for AS ABOVE

service

This section to be completed by the court

To the plaintiff / defendant

Take notice that this application will be heard by the District judge / Judge

at

on   at   o'clock

If you do not attend the Court will make such order that it thinks fit

The court office at

Fig. 5. Notice of application for reissue (form N244).
(Reproduced with permission of HMSO.)

your debtor has taken. If your customer fails to respond to the summons it is your responsibility to follow the action through and apply for judgement. The court will not do this for you.

DEALING WITH NON-SERVICE

It has been assumed you undertook the pre-summons enquiries correctly. What would happen if you had quoted the wrong address for the defendant or they had moved away? Obviously the post office or bailiff will return the summons to the court with a report stating the defendant had 'gone away'. The court will inform you by sending from N216 'Notice of Non-service'. You now have four months from the date you commenced proceedings to locate your debtor and reissue the summons. Unless the defendant receives the summons within this time span you will forfeit the court fees paid, and you must start the action all over again.

Re-check your facts

It is important you have the correct information about your debtor before you start issuing proceedings. Use of customer application forms and pre-sue searches can never be over-emphasised. They lead to better use of your firm's time and resources, which are essential for the continuing growth and profitability of your business.

So what can you do if your summons has not been served? You must:

- confirm the address you entered on form N1 is correct

- call at the defendant's address to check they have in fact moved

- ask the debt or credit agency to corroborate their report.

Immediately you have validated your customer's new address you must make an application to the court to reissue the summons.

APPLYING TO REISSUE YOUR SUMMONS

If for any reason you are unable to reissue the summons in the specified time you can make an application to the court for further time to be granted. It is advisable to make application to the court as early as possible. A sample form of application is given in Figure 5. Once you have established the new address of your customer, or confirmed he still remains at the address stated, you can continue your claim. If you find out that your defendant lied about moving away, a description of your customer should accompany your application to reissue the summons.

Is your information accurate?

It will only take a few summons to be issued before you become a familiar face at your local county court. Too many mistakes, withdrawn applications or struck out cases, and you will rapidly lose all credibility with the court and its staff – which could be to your disadvantage. So get it right first time.

Friendly court staff

The court will supply you with all the forms you will require free of charge. You will find the court staff very friendly and helpful. But they are not solicitors, and cannot give you legal advice, or deal with questions like:

- Will I win my case?
- Can the defendant make a counterclaim against me?

QUESTIONS AND ANSWERS

What is a small claim?

It is a claim for £3,000 or less in England and Wales, £1,000 in Northern Ireland, and £750 in Scotland, made through the county court. Most small claims are about money owed but they can be for faulty goods, noisy neighbours, in fact almost anything.

Where can I start my claim?

In your local county court. The addresses and telephone numbers are listed in the telephone directory. They are open between 10 am and 4 pm Mondays to Fridays.

How do I pay the court fees?

Either by cash, postal order or cheque. Cheques should be made payable to HM Paymaster General.

Will I need help in filling out the form?

No. Simply heed the instructions given in this chapter and follow the example given in Figure 3.

Is it worth paying for a bailiff to serve the summons?

There is little point in paying any extra, unless you have a special reason for doing so. The court will post the summons to your debtor by first class post. It will be returned by the post office if the defendant has moved away. The court will assume the summons has been served if it has not been returned in 14 days. So if your customer did go away without notifying you, they have only themselves to blame if you get judgement in their absence.

Can they challenge the judgement if this happens?

Yes. The defendants can make an application to the court to have the judgement set aside at any time, the same as you can. They must provide reasonable grounds in support of their request. This is only likely to happen if they have a genuine defence to your claim.

Will the case be heard in my local court?

If the defendant disagrees with your claim normally the case will be transferred to a court closer to your customer's home address. It could mean you travelling a very long way to get judgement. However, if your customer admits to the claim and makes an offer to pay, you must take this point into consideration in deciding whether to accept the offer or not.

CHECKLIST

- Are the debtor's details correct, especially their address?
- Have you completed form N1 in triplicate plus extra copies if more than one defendant?
- Have you paid the correct fees?
- Have you enclosed a stamped, self addressed envelope?
- Have you received a copy of notice N222?
- Have you made a diary note, 15 days hence?

CASE STUDIES

Bill decides to sue by post
After collecting form N1 from his local court, Bill Swift hurriedly fills in the details about his customer and the claim. He posts them

DEBT COLLECTION IN THE COUNTY COURT

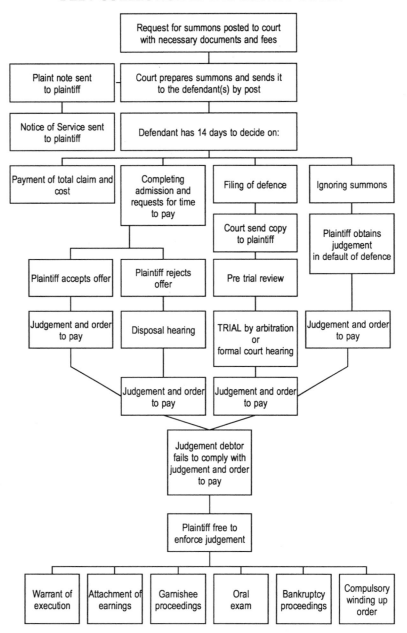

Fig. 6. Charting the course of litigation.

to his local county court with the correct fee and self addressed stamped envelope. In his haste he mistakenly enters the wrong address of the defendant. When he's informed the summons has not been delivered, he checks the details and finds his mistake. He now has to make application to the court for the summons to be re-issued. If he had been a little more careful he might have received payment by now.

Karen double checks her information

Before deciding to go along to her local court personally with the completed form N1 Karen Turner re-checks that all the information she has is correct. A final telephone call confirms Mr Knavish still resides at the address he gave earlier. She hands her forms with the court fee to the nice young man in the court office. He gives the case a plaint number, and before Karen leaves she is given her 'Notice of Issue'. Returning to her office, Karen Turner makes a note in her diary to check with the court in 15 days' time.

Ted sends a cheque

When he receives a summons from the court, Ted Knavish reads the information on the back of the form. This tells him further costs could be added to the claim if judgement is entered against him. It also explains the consequences of having a county court judgement registered against him. Deciding he cannot keep his suppliers waiting any longer and not wanting a judgement registered against his name, which would affect his future credit applications, he sends off a cheque for the full amount claimed, plus the court costs for issuing the summons by return of post. Ted sends the money direct to the plaintiff, as at this stage in the proceedings the court will not accept any money on the plaintiff's behalf. Once his cheque has been cleared, Karen or Bill will inform the court promptly and the matter is at an end.

DISCUSSION POINTS

1. How easy would it be for you to travel if the case is transferred to your debtor's home town?

2. Are you comfortable with the idea of going to court?

3. What level of debt would you think not worth recovering?

4
Getting Judgement

MAKING AN APPLICATION FOR JUDGEMENT

There are a number of things you must do before making an application for judgement, depending on whether the defendant ignored the summons or made an offer to pay.

Fifteen days later

Now the fifteenth day has elapsed since the 'Notice of issue' form N222 and N205 or N205A (see Figure 7) told you the date your summons against the defendant was posted or delivered. Now you must enquire at the court if your customer responded to the summons. Whether you go along to the court, telephone or write to them always quote the 'plaint or case number' given to you by the court staff. You will not be prompted, it is your responsibility to ask for judgement if the defendant has not responded to the summons.

Default summons

Throughout this book you will see samples of forms you will have to complete, and forms you or the defendant will receive from the court. Only those forms which you must complete to issue or obtain judgement have been filled out. The others are for information and identification purposes only, so you will be familiar with them when they arrive on your doormat. On some forms reference is made to either a fixed or non-fixed amount summons: only the fixed amount forms are illustrated and explained. It is this type of summons you will be most concerned with, but let me explain the differences.

Fixed amount summons

This is the most common form of default summons (form N205A): used for monetary claims such as trade debts, where you are aware of the exact amount of money due to you.

Non-fixed summons

For claims in which you are not aware of the amount you are claiming – asking for damages for example, and you want the court to determine the sum. Form N205 would be used in this case.

Entering judgement by default

If the debtor has done nothing since receiving the summons you must now make an application to the court for judgement by default. Your application is simply a request for the court to send the defendant an order to pay what is owed to you. For judgement to be entered simply complete the 'Request for judgement' section on form N205A by placing a tick in box A. Before completing the form you must do two or three things:

- calculate the amount of interest to be added to your claim

- decide when you want the defendant to pay

- how you want them to pay, in full or by instalments.

To complete the tear off portion of form N205A marked request for judgement, first tick box A.

The defendant admits your claim

If your customer agrees with your claim, you must tick box B before ticking one of the following boxes:

Box 1.   If the defendant has made an offer to pay, which you wish to accept.

Box 2.   If your customer admits your claim but does not make an offer to pay.

Box 3.   If they have made an offer to pay that you do not wish to accept.

If your customer has not made an offer to pay or you intend to decline a defendant's offer, your reasons for doing so can be stated on the space provided on the reverse of this form. Copies of any evidence you have relating to the defendant's means and income should be forwarded to the court. On the other hand if you are accepting your debtor's offer of instalments form N205A acts as a request to the court to 'enter judgement on acceptance'.

Notice of Issue of Default Summons – fixed amount

N205A 387

To the plaintiff ('s solicitor)

> EDWARD KNAVISH
> T/A KNAVISH & Co
> NEW TOWN ST
> ANY TOWN   2X1 1X2

Your summons was issued today. The defendant has 14 days from the date of service to reply to the summons. If the date of postal service is not shown on this form you will be sent a separate notice of service (Form N222).

The defendant may either

- Pay you your total claim.
- **Dispute the whole claim.** The court will send you a copy of the defence and tell you what to do next.
- **Admit that all the money is owed.** The defendant will send you form of admission N9A. You may then ask the court to send the defendant an order to pay you the money owed by completing the request for judgment below and returning it to the court.
- **Admit that only part of your claim is owed.** The court will send you a copy of the reply and tell you what to do next.
- **Not reply at all.** You should wait 14 days from the date of service. You may then ask the court to send the defendant an order to pay you the money owed by completing the request for judgment below and returning it to the court.

In the

ANY TOWN   County Court

The court office at

ESSEX RM1 4DP
is open between 10 am & 4 pm Monday to Friday

Case Number	Always quote this	123

Plaintiff (including ref.)

WILLIAM SWIFT

Defendants

EDWARD KNAVISH

Issue date	
Date of postal service	
Issue fee	£

For further information please turn over

Request for Judgment

- Tick and complete either A or B. Make sure that all the case details are given and that the judgment details at C are completed. Remember to sign and date the form. Your signature certifies that the information you have given is correct.
- If the defendant has given an address on the form of admission to which correspondence should be sent, which is different from the address shown on the summons, you will need to tell the court.

A ☐ **The defendant has not replied to my summons**

Complete all the judgment details at C. Decide how and when you want the defendant to pay. You can ask for the judgment to be paid by instalments or in one payment.

B ☑ **The defendant admits that all the money is owed**

Tick only **one** box below and return the completed slip to the court.

☑ **I accept the defendant's proposal for payment**

Complete all the judgment details at C. Say how the defendant intends to pay. The court will send the defendant an order to pay. You will also be sent a copy.

☐ **The defendant has not made any proposal for payment**

Complete all the judgment details at C. Say how you want the defendant to pay. You can ask for the judgment to be paid by instalments or in one payment. The court will send the defendant an order to pay. You will also be sent a copy.

☐ **I do NOT accept the defendant's proposal for payment**

Complete all the judgment details at C and say how you want the defendant to pay. Give your reasons for objecting to the defendant's offer of payment in the section overleaf. Return this slip to the court **together with the defendant's admission N9A** (or a copy). The court will fix a rate of payment and send the defendant an order to pay. You will also be sent a copy.

I certify that the information given is correct

Signed   *W. Swift*   Dated 17/12/ax

In the **ANY TOWN**   County Court

Case Number	Always quote this	123

Plaintiff   W. SWIFT

Defendant   EDWARD KNAVISH

Plaintiff's Ref.

C   Judgment details

I would like the judgment to be paid

☐ (forthwith only in £ this box if you intend to enforce the order right away)

☑ (by instalments of £ **100.00**   per month)

☐ (in full **by**)

Amount of claim as stated in summons (including interest at date of issue)	2448	00
Interest since date of summons (if any) Period .... Rate ....%		
Court fees shown on summons	65	00
Solicitor's costs (if any) on issuing summons		
Sub Total	2513	00
Solicitor's costs (if any) on entering judgment		
Sub Total		
Deduct amount (if any) paid since issue	100	00
Amount payable by defendant	2413	00

Fig. 7. Notice of issue of summons (N205A).
(Reproduced with permission of HMSO.)

DECIDING HOW YOUR DEFENDANT MUST PAY

In section C on form 205A you will note there are three small boxes – only tick and complete one of them. But before rushing ahead and ticking the first one, give some consideration to the information you received in the pre-sue search. It will be no use demanding unreasonable payments from the defendant. It is far better to agree a figure and be sure of regular reductions on the sum owed than get nothing at all. Spending time and money trying to get blood out of a stone can be frustrating. Remember if it takes a summons to be issued and a judgement to be registered to get your customer to pay, what chance do you have of getting an immediate payment in full?

- Tick the first box only if you are confident the defendant can pay straight away.

- Use the second box if you wish to be paid by instalments.

- The third box is for those cases where you know the defendant will have the means to pay in full at some future date.

Knowing as much as possible about your customer and their finances is essential. Using a good credit reference agency can be money well spent. When returning the lower section of form N205A to the court, if you are challenging the defendant's offer of payment the pre-sue search you obtained makes excellent evidence to support your request for a higher payment.

CALCULATING YOUR INTEREST

Interest can now be levied on all claims. For claims less than £5,000 interest is only allowable from the date of issue of the summons until the date of judgement. Interest on sums in excess of £5,000 can be charged up to the date of settlement, providing judgement was obtained for the full sum of the claim to be paid by a fixed date. For judgement by agreed instalments, the rules relating to sums below £5,000 apply. When applying for interest in section C of form N205A the notice of issue must accompany the form. In the illustrations we are claiming the sum of £2,432.16p, and interest at the rate of 15 per cent per annum. The calculation will therefore be:

15% of £2,432.16p = £364.82 per annum. Divide this sum by 365 days and this will give you a daily rate of interest of 99p. Multiply this sum by the number of days between the date of the summons being issued and the day you are requesting judgement. Let's say by the time you got to court it was 16 days. The interest you can claim is 99p by 16 = £15.84p. This sum is in addition to the court costs which you can add to the debt.

DEALING WITH AN OFFER TO PAY

When your customer receives the summons, among the papers will be a form N9A (see Figure 8). This form is an admission to the debt either in full or part. In this chapter we shall deal with a full admission. The following chapter deals with both a full and partial defence. The defendant completes the form by inserting the amount they are admitting, then in descending order on both sides of the form will state:

- full personal details
- number of dependants
- details of employment
- bank and savings accounts
- type of property they live in (*ie* rented or owned)
- income from all sources
- items of expenditure
- priority debts, current court orders and credit debts
- when they can pay or the amount of monthly instalments offered.

You will be sent a copy of this form; if it disagrees with your pre-sue search and you do not accept it say so as previously indicated. If you accept the offer, this is referred to as 'entering judgement on acceptance'. If you disagree with what the defendant stated on form N9A you must return your copy of that form to the court when sending the lower portion of form N205A. You must clearly state your reason for not accepting the defendant's plea, together with copies of all supporting evidence in your possession, to back up your argument. Failure to disclose sufficient information could mean you getting a lower judgement figure than you would otherwise be entitled to. At this stage, only send copies of your evidence.

What the court will do

Now you have returned the 'Request for judgement' form to the court, with the mandatory stamped, self addressed envelope. The court will peruse the section of form N205A you returned together with your supporting evidence, alongside your debtor's admission form N9A which he received with his summons and has now returned to the court.

Giving judgement

The court will take into consideration the offer made by the defendant and the information they supplied on Form N9A, weighing this against the reasons and evidence you submitted for not accepting their offer. After careful deliberation the court will decide what would be a fair amount and/or method for the defendant to pay. The court will inform the defendant of their judgement, by sending the defendant either of the following notices, depending on the type of judgement:

N30(1)T   judgement for the plaintiff – on acceptance of offer
N30T   judgement for plaintiff – after a hearing
N30(2)T   judgement for the defendant – by determination
N30(3)T   judgement for plaintiff – in default.

These notices inform and order the defendant:

- how much they must pay

- when to pay

- the address where you want the money sent.

They also inform the defendant what could happen if the instructions are ignored, and the possible consequences for their ability to obtain credit in the future. These directions are explained in the chapters relating to enforcing judgement. These forms are stamped by the court and a copy will be sent to you. If you are not satisfied or disagree in any way with the order given, you can challenge it. You have 16 days from the date of the postmark on the judgement order to make an application to object to the decision. The court will arrange a hearing for you to state your reasons for rejecting the judgement order.

Admission

When to fill in this form

- Only fill in this form if you are admitting all or some of the claim **and** you are asking for time to pay
- If you are disputing the claim or you wish to pay the amount claimed, read the back of the summons

How to fill in this form

- Tick the correct boxes and give as much information as you can. **Then sign and date the form.**
- Make your offer of payment in box 11 on the back of this form. **If you make no offer the plaintiff will decide how you should pay.**
- You can get help to complete this form at **any** county court office or citizens' advice bureau.

Where to send this form

- **If you admit the claim in full**
  Send the completed form to the address shown at box (2) on the front of the summons. If there is no address in box (2) send the form to the address in box (1).
- **If you admit only part of the claim**.
  Send the form **to the court** at the address given on the summons, together with the white defence form (N9B).

What happens next

- **If you admit the claim in full and offer to pay**
  If the plaintiff accepts your offer, judgment will be entered and you will be sent an order telling you how and when to pay. If the plaintiff does **not** accept your offer, the court will fix a rate of payment based on the details you have given in this form and the plaintiff's comments. Judgment will be entered and you will be sent an order telling you how and when to pay.
- **If you admit only part of the claim**
  The court will tell you what to do next.

How much of the claim do you admit?

☐ I admit the full amount claimed as shown on the summons **or**

☐ I admit the amount of   £

---

1 Personal details

Surname

Forename

☐ Mr   ☐ Mrs   ☐ Miss   ☐ Ms

☐ Married   ☐ Single   ☐ Other *(specify)*

Age

Address

Postcode

In the

County Court

Case Number *Always quote this*

Plaintiff *(including ref.)*

Defendant

2 Dependants *(people you look after financially)*

Number of children in each age group

under 11 ____   11-15 ____   16-17 ____   18 & over ____

Other dependants *(give details)*

3 Employment

☐ I am employed as a

My employer is

Jobs other than main job *(give details)*

☐ I am self employed as a

Annual turnover is...................... £

☐ I am not in arrears with my national insurance contributions, income tax and VAT

☐ I am in arrears and I owe.......... £

Give details of:
(a) contracts and other work in hand
(b) any sums due for work done

☐ I have been unemployed for   years   months

☐ I am a pensioner

4 Bank account and savings

☐ I have a bank account

  ☐ The account is in credit by .... £

  ☐ The account is overdrawn by.... £

☐ I have a savings or building society account

  The amount in the account is .... £

5 Property

I live in   ☐ my own property   ☐ lodgings

  ☐ jointly owned property   ☐ council property

  ☐ rented property

Fig. 8. Example of debtor's admission form (N9A).
(Reproduced with permission of HMSO.)

6 Income

My usual take home pay *(including overtime, commission, bonuses etc)*	£	per
Income support	£	per
Child benefit(s)	£	per
Other state benefit(s)	£	per
My pension(s)	£	per
Others living in my home give me	£	per
Other income *(give details below)*		
	£	per
	£	per
	£	per
Total income	**£**	**per**

7 Expenses

(Do not include any payments made by other members of the household out of their own income)

I have regular expenses as follows:

Mortgage *(including second mortgage)*	£	per
Rent	£	per
Council Tax	£	per
Gas	£	per
Electricity	£	per
Water charges	£	per
TV rental and licence	£	per
HP repayments	£	per
Mail order	£	per
Housekeeping, food, school meals	£	per
Travelling expenses	£	per
Children's clothing	£	per
Maintenance payments	£	per
Others *(not court orders or credit debts listed in boxes 9 and 10)*		
	£	per
	£	per
	£	per
Total expenses	**£**	**per**

8 Priority debts
This section is for arrears only. Do not include regular expenses listed in box 7.

Rent arrears	£	per
Mortgage arrears	£	per
Council Tax/Community Charge arrears	£	per
Water charges arrears	£	per
Fuel debts: Gas	£	per
Electricity	£	per
Other	£	per
Maintenance arrears	£	per
Others *(give details below)*		
	£	per
	£	per
Total priority debts	**£**	**per**

9 Court orders

Court	Case No.	£	per

Total court order instalments	**£**	**per**

Of the payments above, I am behind with payments to *(please list)*

10 Credit debts

Loans and credit card debts *(please list)*

	£	per
	£	per
	£	per

Of the payments above, I am behind with payments to *(please list)*

11 Do you wish to make an offer of payment?

- *If you take away the totals of boxes 7, 8 and 9 and the payments you are making in box 10 from the total in box 6 you will get some idea of the sort of sum you should offer. The offer you make should be one you can afford.*

☐ I can pay the amount admitted on _____

or

☐ I can pay by monthly instalments of £ _____

12 Declaration   I declare that the details I have given above are true to the best of my knowledge

Signed _____   Dated _____

Position _____
(firm or company)

Fig. 8 (continued).

QUESTIONS AND ANSWERS

Are the procedures the same for a non-monetary claim?

Yes. Instead of asking the court to award you a fixed sum, the district judge will ask the defendant to do something.

What will happen if I disagree with the ruling?

You'll make an application listing your objection, and a hearing will be arranged using the same methods as for a debt.

How long do I have to apply?

Sixteen days from the date postmarked on the judgement order.

Can only the plaintiff object to a judgement order?

No. The defendants can also make an application if they feel the order the court made was unreasonable.

Will the hearing be at the court where I issued the summons?

Only if the defendant lives in the area covered by your local court. If they are outside the court's jurisdiction the case will be transferred nearer to the defendant. Refusing a defendant's offer, or challenging a judgement order, can waste time. You must take these matters into consideration in addition to their ability to pay when deciding to accept or decline an offer to pay by instalments.

Will the appointment be in open court?

No. It will be an informal meeting with the district judge in his chambers. The only ones who'll be present will be the judge, your customer and yourself. The meeting is congruous to an arbitration hearing, which is clarified in a later chapter. You and the debtor will both have an opportunity to query the court's earlier ruling. These appointments are generally referred to as disposal hearings.

Will we wait long for the new judgement order?

No. After reading all the various forms and items of evidence submitted by the defendant and yourself, the district judge will listen to what you both have to say. He or she will make a new ruling and explain the motive for his or her decision before you leave the court.

CHECKLIST

It is the fifteenth day since the summons was issued. Have you:

- completed form N205A and sent it to the court
- applied for judgement to be entered by default
- calculated the interest (if applicable)
- accepted an offer of payment
- decided when you require judgement to be paid, and where
- confirmed the details submitted on form N9A tally with your pre-sue search
- decided to accept or to object to the amount of the judgement awarded?

CASE STUDIES

Bill challenges the court's ruling

Not content with the decision of the district judge, Bill Swift makes an application for a hearing. He does not intend to wait any longer for Mr Knavish to pay what is owed. He considers the information given by his customer on form N9A to be false. The pre-sue search indicated Mr Knavish made a profit last year, but because it is over six months since his accounts were filed, they did not record his business taking a dive, so during this period his income was much lower than in the previous year.

After making an application, Bill receives a date for the hearing. If he fails to turn up the application will be thrown out, and the earlier order will stand. If Mr Knavish did not arrive for the appointment the district judge will hear what Bill has to say, consider his evidence and fix judgement in Mr Knavish's absence.

On the day of the hearing both Bill and Mr Knavish attend court, and after hearing both parties, and reconsidering the evidence before him, the judge increases Mr Knavish's offer by a pound per week. Bill returns to his business a little disappointed after spending nearly all day in court, and he still has to wait another month before he can get the first payment from Mr Knavish. All for an extra £1 per week.

Karen accepts an offer

After checking the details Mr Knavish gave on form N9A and the information supplied by the credit reference agency, she decided it was not worth arguing about the difference. She completes the appropriate section on form N205A, accepting the amounts offered by her customer. Judgement is entered without Karen attending court and spending time away from the office. Karen's firm receives two payments from Mr Knavish before Bill Swift receives the amended judgement order.

Ted admits defeat

Realising his suppliers are not prepared to wait for payment any longer, Ted carefully reads and follows the instructions which arrived with the summons and submits an offer to pay. Careful to itemise every detail of his income and expenditure accurately, he is irked when Bill Swift refuses to accept the court's judgement. He must lose a day's income to attend court, which he can barely afford.

DISCUSSION POINTS

1. What are the disadvantages if you refuse to accept a defendant's offer?

2. Could you have done anything to avoid issuing a summons?

3. What interest could you claim on a judgement debt of less than £5,000?

5
Dealing with a Defence

REMOVING CAUSE

Normally with most claims for money owed, such as a trade debt, the actions are uncomplicated. Knavish & Co places an order, the goods are delivered, Mr Knavish or his son checks the delivery, and if satisfied signs a consignment or delivery note clearly stating the goods were received and inspected. Any shortages or breakages are noted and recorded on the delivery note. This document is signed by Mr Knavish and the driver. A copy of the note with any amendments signed by both parties is retained by the customer. The entire transaction is fully documented and easily proved.

A matter of prudence
It is advisable for your customer to report to you any discrepancies found at the time and point of delivery. A simple note or telephone call to your accounts or despatch department will suffice. Unfortunately life is not always as simple and straightforward as we would like, and customers do not always act as you would wish them to.

Preparing invoices
Notice of delivery problems by your customer or driver allows you to prepare and send your customer an invoice as per your normal procedures. There should be time to adjust the invoice and allow for any changes entered on the delivery note to be verified. If your firm sends an invoice with the order it is up to you to check there are no mistakes. If errors are brought to light after an invoice has been handed to your customer, you should, after confirming the mistakes, issue a credit note. Do not wait for your customers to complain. Speedy action on your part can remove a reason for non-payment by your customer; it shows your customer you care, and ensures you are paid on time.

Defence and Counterclaim

<table>
<tr><td>In the</td></tr>
</table>

	County Court

Case Number	*Always quote this*	

Plaintiff *(including ref.)*	

Defendant	

The court office is open from 10am to 4pm Monday to Friday

When to fill in this form
* Only fill in this form if you wish to dispute all or part of the claim **and/or** make a claim against the plaintiff (counterclaim).

How to fill in this form
* Please check that the correct case details are shown on this form. You must ensure that all the boxes at the top right of this form are completed. You can obtain the correct names and numbers from the summons. The court cannot trace your case without this information.
* Follow the instructions given in each section. Tick the correct boxes and give the other details asked for.
* If you wish only to make a claim against the plaintiff (counterclaim) go to section 5.
* Complete and sign section 6 before returning this form.

Where to send this form
* Send or take this form immediately to the court office at the address shown above.
* If you admit part of the claim and you are asking for time to pay, you will also need to fill in the blue admission form (N9A) and send **both** reply forms to the court.
* Keep the summons and a copy of this defence; you may need them.

Legal Aid
* You may be entitled to legal aid. Ask about the legal aid scheme at any county court office, Citizens Advice Bureau, legal advice centre or firm of solicitors displaying the legal aid sign.

What happens next
* If you complete box 3 on this form, the court will ask the plaintiff to confirm that he has received payment. If he tells the court that you have not paid, the court will tell you what you should do.
* If you complete box 4 or 5, the court will tell you what you should do.
* If the summons is not from your local county court, it will automatically be transferred to your local court.

1 How much of the claim do you dispute?

I dispute the full amount claimed *(go to section 2)*

or

I admit the amount of £

If you dispute only part of the claim you must **either**:

* pay the amount admitted to the person named at the address for payment in box (2) on the front of the summons or if there is no address in box (2), send the money to the address in box (1) (see How to Pay on the back of the summons). Then send this defence to the court.

or
* complete the blue admission form and this defence form and send them to the court.

Tick whichever applies

I paid the amount admitted on *(date)*

or

I enclose the completed form of admission
(go to section 2)

2 Arbitration under the small claims procedure
How the claim will be dealt with if defended

If the total the plaintiff is claiming is £3,000 or less, it will be dealt with by arbitration (small claims procedure) unless the court decides the case is too difficult to be dealt with in this informal way. Costs and the grounds for setting aside an arbitration award are strictly limited. If the claim is not dealt with by arbitration, costs, including the costs of help from a legal representative, may be allowed.

If the total the plaintiff is claiming is more than £3,000, it can still be dealt with by arbitration if you or the plaintiff ask for it and the court approves. If your claim is dealt with by arbitration in these circumstances, costs may be allowed.

Please tick this box if you would like the claim dealt with by arbitration.
(go on to section 3)

3 Do you dispute this claim because you have already paid it? *Tick whichever applies*

No *(go to section 4)*

Yes I paid £   to the plaintiff

on   *(before the summons was issued - see summons)*

Give details of where and how you paid it in the box below *(then go to section 6)*

Fig. 9. Form for defence and counterclaim (N9B).
(Reproduced with permission of HMSO.)

60

Case No. [ ]

4 **If you dispute the claim for reasons other than payment, what are your reasons?**

Use the box below to give full details *(If you need to continue on a separate sheet, put the case number in the top right hand corner)*

[ ]

5 **If you wish to make a claim against the plaintiff (counterclaim)**

If your claim is for a specific sum of money, how much are you claiming?

£ [ ]

- If your claim against the plaintiff is for more than the plaintiff's claim against you, you may have to pay a fee. Ask at your local court office whether a fee is payable.

- You may not be able to make a counterclaim where the plaintiff is the Crown (eg a Government Department). Ask at your local county court office for further information.

What are your reasons for making the counterclaim?

- Use the box opposite to give full details.
  (If you need to continue on a separate sheet, put the case number in the top right hand corner.)

(go on to section 6)

6 **Signed**

(To be signed by you or by your solicitor)

Position
(if signing on behalf of firm or company)

Give an address to which notices about this case can be sent to you

Postcode [ ]

Dated

Fig. 9. (continued).

61

DEALING WITH A DEFENDANT'S COUNTERCLAIM OR DEFENCE

There should be no grounds remaining for a counterclaim or defence to be lodged. It is assumed your customer will check the contents of the invoice on receipt. The debt is now clearly documented and easily proven. There are absolutely no grounds remaining to justify a defence or counterclaim to be filed against you. Or are there?

So what can go wrong?

The defendant disagrees with either part or the whole of your claim. Your customer amended the delivery note to show the delivery was short. But unfortunately you omitted to send a credit note. Because of an error by someone in your firm the defendant has a genuine counterclaim against you. So in addition to form N9A, the defendant completes and returns form N9B (Figure 9). Again this must be returned to the court within 14 days of receipt. A copy of your customer's defence or counterclaim will be sent to you by the court. It is now up to you what you do next; you can either:

1. Accept the defendant's part admission, after checking the defendant's statement on form N9B with your internal records. If in agreement you will inform the court by completing form N205A as explained in the previous chapter.

2. Disagree with their defence statement to either all or part of your claim, in which case you must inform the court by stating your reasons on form N244 (Figure 5 in Chapter 3).

The method of dealing with these situations requires the completion of the forms described in Chapter 4. If you agree with what your customer has stated, the court will deal with the forms in exactly the same manner as earlier explained. But if you disagree entirely with the defendant's part claim, the action will continue as if the defendant had submitted a full defence against your lawsuit.

ATTENDING A PRELIMINARY HEARING

So, the defendant does not admit to your claim. If in fact Knavish & Co believe they have a valid counterclaim against you, they would complete either the defence or defence and counterclaim section on form N9B and return it to the court within the obligatory 14 days. A copy of their defence and details of any counterclaim will be forwarded to you.

In the meantime

Back at the court, your case file will be passed to a district judge. He or she will study your claim, Knavish & Co's defence to that claim, and any counterclaim they feel they are entitled to. The district judge will decide what happens next. If either the defendant or yourself have given insufficient information on the respective forms for the judge to make a decision, he or she will wish to question both of you. To do this he must fix a date for a preliminary hearing. The court staff will notify you by using form N18 'Notice of a preliminary hearing'.

Notice of a preliminary hearing

The court will inform you about the preliminary hearing by using form N18 (not illustrated). This is a simple form of instructions, which will state the case number and date, the defendant's and plaintiff's names and any reference either of you gave to the court earlier. The form will tell you:

- the date of the appointment (there is usually a six week delay)

- the time and place to attend

- about the preliminary appointment

- what will happen after the hearing

- the outcome if you fail to attend.

The main aim of the hearing is to make sure all parties know what the claim is about. Also it will try and resolve the dispute. If not, it will decide how the matter can be dealt with, and how long the case will take. At the hearing you will be informed about what other documents or evidence will be needed at the next hearing.

Using a 'lay representative'

You can take someone with you to the hearing to speak for you. This is referred to in court as a 'right of audience'. To request a lay representative to attend the hearing with you, form EX83 must be completed and sent to the court as early as possible. An example of how to fill out this form is shown in Figure 10. The person you

Notice of Lay Representative

Fill in the form. Take it with you to the hearing and hand it to the district judge.

Plaintiff

WILLIAM SWIFT

Defendant

EDWARD KNAVISH

In the	
ANY TOWN	County Court
Case No.	123
Date:	30 / 11 / 9X

To the court

A   To be completed by the plaintiff or defendant

I am the   plaintiff ☑   defendant ☐   in the above case.

A hearing is to take place

at   ANY TOWN COUNTY COURT, LAW ST, ANY TOWN

on   2 ND DECEMBER 199X   at 10 o'clock AM

I am bringing a lay representative with me to that hearing.

The lay representative is   (a) a relative ☐   if so, give relationship

(b) a friend ☑   (c) a voluntary advice worker *(the service is free)* ☐

(d) a professional adviser *(you are paying for the service)* ☐

If you have ticked box (c) or (d) say what kind of organisation the person belongs to *e.g. citizens advice bureau, trade union, accountancy business, etc*

The name of the lay representative is: ROBIN SWALLOW
of (address)   14, BIRDNEST ST ANY TOWN

If you ticked box (c) or (d) above also give the name of organisation and its business or office address

B   To be completed by the district judge.

The name of the district judge is

Was the lay representative excluded from the hearing ?   No ☐   Yes ☐
If YES, specify the conduct which warranted the exclusion:

———— Note for Court Staff ————

Where the box above is completed send a copy of this form to   Civil Business 'A'

Fig. 10. Notice of a lay representative (EX83).
(Reproduced with permission of HMSO.)

choose to take along, known as a 'lay representative', can be anyone you like, such as:

- your spouse
- a relative or friend
- an advice worker.

Choosing a lay person

A lay representative may wish to be paid for helping you; the amount should be clarified as soon as possible so you will know exactly how much this will be. Paying for a lay representative is not an allowable cost, and the court will not charge this to the defendant if you win your case. When appointing a lay representative carefully weigh up the cost, and remember if a lay representative wrongly advises you or makes a mistake you could lose your case, and have no retribution against this person. If the district judge thinks your lay representative is behaving badly, he can order him or her to leave at any time. Witnesses will not be called at a preliminary hearing.

What a lay representative cannot do

Lay representatives cannot attend any court hearings on their own, you must accompany them. Neither do they have the right to conduct litigation on your behalf, so the party to the action must sign all pleadings, and be in attendance at all hearings. Salaried members of your staff are not classified as lay representatives, and can attend on your behalf, providing they have your authority to make decisions.

Objecting to a preliminary hearing

If you do not wish to use this procedure for dealing with your claim, you can make application to the court using form N224, as described earlier. You must state why you object, and what form you wish the claim to take. The court will give you an appointment at which the district judge will consider your objection. You can in fact make an application to the court at any time. This is called 'asking for leave', and can be used to ask the court or defendant to do anything such as:

- produce further evidence
- adjourn the proceedings
- bring an extra witness.

But whenever you take an application to the court and you receive a date for a hearing turn up at the court as ordered. Failure to attend will result in your request being thrown out, and if you eventually lose the case extra costs could be awarded to your customer.

After the preliminary hearing

You will be sent form 18A and N18AX: this is a notice of an arbitration hearing. It will tell you:

- the outcome of the preliminary hearing
- what you must do to prepare for an arbitration hearing
- the time, date and place of the arbitration hearing
- how long it is expected to last
- the purpose of the arbitration hearing.

The form used will be, as for N18, an instructional one. These instructions are referred to as 'directions'. Proceedings at both the preliminary and arbitration hearings are alike. What to do and how to act at these hearings is covered in the following chapter.

GATHERING SUPPORTING EVIDENCE

It could be that the district judge is asking you to take along further evidence in support of your claim. Or maybe he requested Knavish & Co to bring along an expert witness so he or she can understand the true nature of the dispute – this will especially apply when broken machinery is involved in a counterclaim. How to introduce a witness is covered in a later chapter. The evidence you will be requested to bring along with you can be in many forms, but in the case of a claim for non-payment of a trade debt it usually includes:

- copies of all correspondence passed between you both
- perhaps a computer print-out or the actual sales ledger
- examples of your invoices or other documents which display your terms of trade
- actual delivery or despatch notes.

Trial in open court

A decision for a trial in open court can be made either when the district judge sees your file for the first time, or at the disposal hearing. It could be because what transpired at either the preliminary or arbitration hearing gave cause for the matter to be referred to a full hearing. When this decision is made, you will both be notified and given an opportunity to object. How to conduct yourself at a full trial is covered in Chapter 7.

QUESTIONS AND ANSWERS

Can I stop the proceedings?

Yes, if you and the defendant agree. When preparing for the hearing you may locate a missing payment for example. Maybe the defendant states he sent payment, but you claimed never to have received it, or perhaps the defendant improves their offer which you now want to accept. At any time during the case you may make an application to the court withdrawing your action, or accept an improved offer of payment.

Do all cases go to arbitration?

No. It is possible a judgement could be reached at the preliminary hearing, or before if the district judge orders a full trial. He or she could refer the case to the high court if it would be in the interest of either the defendant or yourself.

Do all plaintiffs pay fees?

The initial fees are always paid by the person issuing the summons. However, these can be waived if the plaintiff is on 'income support'. This waiver is at the court's discretion and the request must be made at the time a summons is issued. Proof of 'income support' will be required, such as a payment book.

What costs can I claim?

Fees for issuing the summons, pre-sue reports and searches are allowable, as are telephone, postage and any other expenses the court deems reasonable. All costs are only awarded at the court's discretion and are not obligatory.

Are the full costs always allowed?

Time related costs are never allowed, unless it is for the services of a solicitor. If the judgement awarded by the district judge is lower than the original claim, the costs allowed would be reduced pro rata.

Should the defendant's counterclaim exceed your claim the costs of the case could be awarded against you, the plaintiff.

Must I attend the hearing?

Yes. Either you or a representative member of your staff must attend at the time of the hearing. Failure to attend could mean your case will be struck out. Should something unexpected and important arise, you can of course make an application to the court to adjourn the hearing to a later date.

CHECKLIST

Have you:

- taken steps to prevent a defence
- carried out the directions given by the judge
- prepared your evidence
- studied the full details of the debtor's defence
- worked out what questions to ask
- acquainted yourself with the address of the court?

CASE STUDIES

Bill wants a full trial

Disagreeing with every aspect of Mr Knavish's defence, Bill Swift makes an application for the case to be heard in open court. Completing form N244 'Notice of application' he quotes as his reason for the request the part of the defence he disagrees with. In addition he could add in support of his argument that he wishes to call a witness. The judge considers Bill's application and concludes a trial in open court will serve the best interests of all concerned and grants the request. Ted Knavish receives a copy of the application and as he has no objection to Bill's application, does not bother to attend on the day the application is heard. In his absence the court sets a date for the full trial hearing.

Karen wonders about using a lay representative

Still a little bewildered about the procedure at a preliminary hearing Karen enquires about using a lay representative. She is fearful of getting tongue-tied and asking all the wrong questions. The staff at the court are very helpful and explain that a preliminary hearing is basically an informal meeting of three people. If she is not sure how to put questions to the defendant or the type of questions to ask, the district judge will advise her, and will if requested put any questions she wishes to ask to the defendant on her behalf. This information puts Karen's mind at ease and she decides against a lay representative.

Ted is confident he has a defence

When a delivery was made to Ted's small yard by Karen's firm, he checked the goods before signing the delivery note. Finding only eleven sacks of compost instead of the twelve he ordered, he told the driver, who amended the delivery note and they both signed the alteration. But when the invoice arrived he found he was still being charged for twelve sacks. So he telephoned Karen's office, and refused to pay until he received a credit note. Unfortunately when the delivery note arrived back at the depot the young lady who usually input all the information to the system was on holiday, the temp inadvertently pressed the wrong key and Ted received an incorrect invoice. He telephoned Karen's office, but alas Karen was at lunch; he left a message, but it was mislaid. No one had bothered to check Ted's invoice before it was sent, so he considers he has a partial defence to Karen's claim.

DISCUSSION POINTS

1. What do you think are the pros and cons of using a lay representative?

2. How confident are you that your debtors could never make a valid counterclaim?

6
Going to Arbitration

CHOOSING AN ARBITRATOR

The arbitrator appointed to the majority of court arbitration hearings is normally the district judge. Depending on the nature of the case you can make application to the court to appoint a specialist as arbitrator. This may be because the claim is of a highly technical nature. To request a special arbitrator you will need the agreement of the defendant. There will be an extra cost for appointing someone other than the district judge; this cost will be shared between your debtor and you.

Non-court arbitration

Basically this chapter relates to an arbitration hearing within the small claims court system. It is possible for you and your debtor to agree to a private third party arbitrator. The same applies in a non-debt dispute. How to locate an independent arbitrator is given in the Useful Addresses section. The fees for non-court arbitration can be very high depending on the amount and nature of the claim. The private arbitrators you can call upon fall into three main categories:

1. Trade association arbitrators.
2. Ombudsmen.
3. Industry regulators.

The last two can only be approached when all other negotiations have failed. They are also restricted to working in a single type of service or industry, and cannot be used for private disputes or trade debts.

Trade association arbitrators

As with the ombudsman and regulators there is usually no charge. These are referred to as conciliation schemes, and costs are borne by the trader or the trade association. Some trade associations may, however, ask for a small registration fee, which is normally returned if you win your argument. The disadvantages of this form of solution are that the firm with which you have a dispute must belong to a trade association, and also:

- a trader can leave the association

- you cannot go to court once you have agreed to this type of arbitration

- compensation is not guaranteed.

CALLING AN EXPERT WITNESS

Evidence from a witness can be either oral or written. If you wish to take the first option you must decide early in the proceedings, in order that the witness you will be calling can adjust his or her schedule. Also the court may wish to adjust the length of time the hearing will take. Alternatively it is possible only to use a written statement. A copy of the statement must be sent to the court before the hearing, and a further copy sent to the defendant. Either the district judge or your customer may want to ask questions about the statement. In these cases the witness must be present, as the questions asked may be too difficult for you to answer. You, the plaintiff, are responsible for paying the witness's costs and travel expenses. It is unlikely these will be awarded in a small claim.

Saving time and money

It is feasible to save time and money if you and the defendant agree the evidence of the witness in advance. But this is not essential. To do this simply send two copies of all reports or statements of your proposed witness to the other party, asking them if they will agree with the evidence. This must be done in writing. If they do agree, copies of the evidence must be sent to the court together with the copy of the letter from the defendant confirming their agreement to the report. If you both require an expert witness to give evidence, to reduce the high costs involved there is nothing to stop you asking the defendant to use the same expert. If they are agreeable you can share the costs of providing all the reports you need. It is important to remember the report must be signed and dated, otherwise it will not be allowed as evidence.

The hearing

The previous chapter mentioned similarities between the preliminary and arbitration hearings. Both hearings are:

- informal
- held in chambers.

The basic difference between the two hearings is that at the preliminary hearing a witness will not be allowed to give evidence. The only people present will be:

- the district judge
- you, the plaintiff
- the defendant.

In chambers

As you enter chambers, you will be shown to a table. First stand behind your chairs: you will be on one side of the table, your customer on the other. When the arbitrator enters the room and takes his or her seat at the head of the table, you may both sit. The arbitrator will be addressed as 'Sir' or 'Madam' throughout the hearing, and you will remain seated at all times. If either of you have called witnesses they will be sitting on the appropriate sides of the table. In front of you should be the evidence you brought with you, in the order it will be required.

PRESENTING YOUR CASE

First, as the plaintiff you will be asked to state your case. Slowly, clearly and in a confident manner you should in this order:

1. Identify yourself by stating your name, address and occupation.
2. Declare the amount you are claiming.
3. State why you are owed the money.
4. Explain how the debt arose.
5. Describe the steps you took to obtain payment and to avoid issuing a summons.

During the time you are speaking the arbitrator may, if unsure of any details, ask you questions. The defendant will not be allowed to question your statement until after you have finished putting your case. Next the defendant will be requested to put forward his reasons for disagreeing with your claim. Apart from identifying themselves the defendant will:

- tell the court why he should not pay what is claimed

- say what was done to settle the matter

• explain how he thinks the dispute arose, and what he wants to achieve.

Before ending the hearing

The arbitrator will give you an opportunity to question the defendant once he has finished. He will ask to see the supporting evidence from you both. Any witnesses will be questioned by the arbitrator, and you will be given a chance to refute their evidence. Before ending the hearing you will be given a further opportunity to add anything which you may have omitted earlier, or to debate the points raised by the defendant or during the arbitrator's questioning. When all the evidence relating to the matter in hand is presented, and the questioning finished, the arbitrator will end the hearing and announce his decision.

Making an award

On conclusion of the hearing, the arbitrator will deliberate on the evidence submitted and what has been said. After summing up, he or she will either make an award and enter judgement, or if insufficient evidence was submitted, and a statement was made by one of the parties which had not previously been mentioned, he or she might order an adjournment for further witnesses to be called or refer the case to a full trial.

Challenging the decision

You will be told of the arbitrator's conclusion before you leave the hearing. This will be confirmed in writing in the normal manner. It is advisable to take notes throughout the hearing, because the arbitrator and the court staff are only human and they can make mistakes. If you disagree with what the arbitrator ordered or if the notice the court sends you differs from the order stated by the arbitrator you can make an application to challenge the award.

REQUESTING AN ADJOURNMENT

You, the defendant or the district judge can request an adjournment at any stage of the proceedings. It can be before a hearing or during an actual open trial, arbitration or preliminary hearing. If it is before a hearing date, you must apply as early as possible, using form N244 (notice of application as shown in Figure 5).

Making an application to the court

Whether your application is for an adjournment, reissuing a summons or any other reason, always enquire at the court you will be using for their procedure. Some courts will send the application to the defendant, others will require you to do it. Always send the defendant's copy by recorded delivery so if necessary you can prove to the court that the application was posted. Remember to send extra copies of the application to all the defendants if there are more than one – of course do not forget yourself and the court.

Stating your reasons for the adjournment

A valid reason, backed with solid evidence, will be required for serious consideration to be given to your request. Otherwise an adjournment can inconvenience the court and the other parties to the action. An application will be dismissed if you, for example:

- want to see your favourite football team play
- go away on holiday or short break
- want to take your car for a service.

On the other hand, it will be granted if:

- you are summoned to appear before a higher court on the same day
- a close member of your family becomes ill
- there are circumstances beyond your control, a strike for example.

QUESTIONS AND ANSWERS

How many witnesses can I call?

Any reasonable number to prove your case can attend the hearing. But to reduce costs, if more than one witness is necessary, you can take one witness to the court with you and have written statements or reports from the others. The witness in attendance could read the reports to the court.

If a witness refuses to come to court what can I do?

A witness summons can be used to make them attend court and give evidence. You will be responsible for all the witness's costs and expenses, including the time spent on your report, attending at the court, and travel expenses to and from the court.

What must I do to summon a witness?

The court where the hearing will be heard will give you the witness summons forms. A word of warning: if it takes a summons to get your witness to court they will not be very co-operative. Enquire locally for another expert witness, one who will be happy to attend on your behalf and give evidence.

What type of evidence will the expert witness give?

The witness you require in a civil action is not the same as for a criminal case. Evidence in your case could be about faulty equipment, cost of damage or the repairs needed to make a vehicle roadworthy. So you are not restricted in who you use as your witness.

If I summon my witness how much notice must I give?

You should issue your witness summons at least seven days before the hearing. If you are able to issue the summons earlier do so, it will give the witness more time to prepare their report.

What will happen if I don't take a witness but the arbitrator feels one is necessary?

During the hearing, if the arbitrator thinks an expert witness will be advantageous in reaching a fair judgement he will ask for one to be called. This will require the hearing to be adjourned, and another date set. Think carefully on the subject of using a witness: adjournments cost time and money.

CHECKLIST

- Take adequate evidence with you to the hearing.
- Make sure any witness vital to your case will arrive on time.
- Make notes throughout the hearing.
- Avoid adjournments whenever possible.

CASE STUDIES

Bill's case is transferred to a full trial
After reading Bill Swift's claim and Ted Knavish's defence, the arbitrator asks both of them questions, as he is unsure about some of the technical points raised when they gave evidence. Mr

Knavish's defence to Bill's claim relates to part of the equipment he hired not working. Bill on the other hand tells the arbitrator every bit of his equipment is checked and serviced before it leaves his yard. The arbitrator questions Bill about servicing the machinery. Bill explains that he employs a mechanic to do these chores. The arbitrator then asks Bill if he checks the work. Bill replies he doesn't. Considering the mechanic's testimony is an important part of the evidence, the arbitrator most probably could either adjourn the hearing so Bill's employee could be called, or refer the matter to an open trial. He orders the latter.

Karen is awarded a reduced judgement

Taking insufficient evidence to support her claim, Karen is unable to convince the arbitrator that Ted Knavish received the full load he had ordered. Whilst admitting a shortage of stock meant delivery was in two separate units, she was not aware that one part of the order was unusable. Consequently the arbitrator reduces her claim and awards costs proportionately, in line with his award. With hindsight Karen realises that had she spent more time organising herself and the evidence, the item of unusable stock would have come to light earlier, allowing her and Ted Knavish to reach agreement prior to the hearing (commonly referred to as an 'out of court settlement').

Ted saves his reputation

Having proven to the arbitrator that Karen's claim is incorrect, he accepts the award made by the arbitrator without further argument and agrees to pay Karen's firm the full amount of the award plus the cost of issuing the summons right away. The judgement awarded against him will be listed as satisfied; his credit rating should remain unaffected.

DISCUSSION POINTS

1. What could be the disadvantages of using a trade association arbitrator?

2. Is it worth trying to persuade an obviously unwilling witness to support your case?

7
Your Day in Court

ARRIVING AT COURT

Make sure you arrive early: being late could mean your case will be thrown out. If you are calling a witness, emphasise to him or her the importance of being on time. Ensure you have all the pertinent documents with you which relate to your case.

As you enter the court building your first objective is to discover in which courtroom your case is listed (there can be five or more courtrooms in the building). In most modern court buildings there is usually a reception desk – tell the receptionist your name or company title if suing as a firm, and your plaint number. You will be told the number of the court your case will be heard in, and directed to it. In older courts lists are displayed in the entrance hall. There will be one list per court room. Inspect each list until you find your case number and details, and go along and present yourself to the usher of the court you have been assigned.

Waiting to be heard
Once you have made yourself known to the usher, tell him if you are expecting a witness; he will tell you if they have already arrived or when they turn up. Some of the modern courts have a cafeteria where you can wait. The usher can sometimes indicate how long it will be before your case is heard. If you are attending your first hearing, you might find it helpful to sit at the back of the courtroom to hear how other cases are dealt with. You will become familiar with the court's procedures and thereby give your confidence a boost.

Tell the usher where you'll be
If you decide to wait anywhere other than in or just outside the courtroom always inform the usher where you will be. If the cases before yours are settled early, and your case is called but nobody knows where you are, you can lose your case – and all because of a sudden call of nature, for example.

CONDUCTING YOURSELF IN COURT

Entering the courtroom you will notice an air of formality which was not evident at either the preliminary or arbitration hearings. The district judge is now wearing a wig and gown. Any counsel present will also be wigged and gowned. The usher, who will now be standing in front of the bench, will say something like, 'Will the court please rise'. He then informs the judge who enters the courtroom and takes his seat at the bench. Out of respect everyone present bows their heads, and will not sit until the judge has taken his seat.

Taking the oath

The court usher will call your case, and you will be requested to step into the witness box. You will take with you all the evidence to support your claim. Approaching you in the witness box the usher will enquire of your religious beliefs. You will now be sworn in; if you are not of any religious persuasion you will be asked to 'affirm'. The court is able to cope with all religious tenets. Once you have entered the witness box everything you say, including taking the oath, must be addressed to the judge.

Giving evidence

Stepping into the witness box for the first time can be a daunting experience. Taking two or three deep breaths will help you to overcome any nervousness. Remember to speak slowly, clearly and with deliberation. Before stating the details of your claim you will be asked to identify yourself by disclosing:

- your name
- occupation
- address.

Now you must state the details of your claim.

Stating your case

Tell the judge the amount you are claiming, how the debt arose, and the proof you are offering. For a trade debt this will normally be copy invoices. These must be clearly numbered, and if not stated on the document your terms of trade or any other supporting information should be attached. Most probably the judge will want to see them. Do not hand the documents directly to the judge, but via the usher. Throughout the time you are speaking the judge will be making notes. Whilst you are talking the judge may ask you questions which you must answer honestly and directly at the judge. Your customer will be given time to ask you any questions about your evidence, once you have finished giving testimony.

SELECTING YOUR QUESTIONS

Once you have completed your claim, the defendant will be given an opportunity to put forward his defence, and if appropriate a counterclaim. The procedure will be the same as for you. After he completes his defence you will be able to ask him any questions relating to what he has said. Your questions must:

* be relevant to the case

* relate to the witness or defendant's statement

* refer to facts and not conjecture.

Questioning a defendant's testimony
If your questions are incorrectly put, or are not concerned directly with the facts, the judge will stop and advise you. You will not be allowed to interrupt the defendant whilst he or she is giving testimony. You must wait until they have finished speaking before putting forward any queries. It is important that you make a note of any points you want to raise about what was stated so you can ask for clarification when permitted.

Witness's evidence
If, because of the nature of your claim and your debtor's defence, a witness is being used, he or she will be requested to step into the witness box, take the oath and identify themselves. First they will be shown a copy of the statement or report they made earlier and invited to confirm its accuracy. Both the defendant and the plaintiff can ask questions, in addition to the judge. An expert's evidence is restricted to their area of expertise, and they will not be allowed to make general comments.

Summing up
Now everyone concerned in the case has given his or her evidence, the judge will confirm no one wishes to ask further questions, or make any other statement. He or she will then study the notes made throughout the hearing and the evidence submitted. If any legal

point has arisen during the course of the hearing the judge will have perused the relevant case study. Now the judge gives his judgement, and states his reasoning for reaching the conclusion he has. With a straightforward claim for a trade debt, judgement is synonymous with the summing up of the case.

Taking notes
It is imperative that you take notes of the judge's summing up of the case and the reasons he gave for awarding judgement. These notes will be useful if you consider you have grounds for applying to have the judgement to be set aside or to appeal against the award, at a later date.

That's the easy part over
Having got your judgement, you are now only halfway to getting paid. What if the defendant doesn't pay as ordered? You will need to enforce payment of the judgement. The court will not automatically enforce payment on your behalf. The ball is firmly in your court. It is you, the plaintiff, who must instruct the court on the method of enforcement you wish to use. There are many options of enforcement open to you; what you can do and how to put them into operation are covered in the following chapters.

QUESTIONS AND ANSWERS

Will the cases be heard in the order listed?

Not always. Those hearings where either the plaintiff or defendant or both are represented by lawyers are nearly always given precedence over other non-represented lawsuits.

Can I sit in any hearing if I'm not involved?

Yes. In fact it is advisable before your first hearing. Seeing how other people behave and what they must do will help you to familiarise yourself with the court's routine.

I am frightened of speaking in public – what can I do?

By visiting the court and seeing how other people can be just as scared as you may be will help you overcome your own nerves. Your legs will probably feel like jelly on your first court appearance. Don't worry – the moment you start to speak, you will wonder what all the fuss was about.

What happens if I am not there when my case is called?

If you told the usher you were slipping away for a few seconds, the court will wait. But on the other hand, if you told the usher you would be longer than a few minutes the next case could be brought forward.

What if I forgot to tell the usher where I'd be?

After a very short period if you, the plaintiff, were not present when called, your claim could be dismissed: you would be liable for costs and would need to reissue the summons. If it was the defendant who went away, you would be awarded judgement in their absence.

What should I do if my witness is held up?

If, for example, your witness got held up in traffic or their train was delayed, you must tell the court at once and your case will be put back until later in the day. If they do not turn up at all or get in contact with you, ask for the case to be adjourned to another day.

CHECKLIST

• Is your claim correct?

• Have you examined your evidence for accuracy?

• Have you informed your witness of the date, time and place of the hearing?

• Have you made a list of all the questions you wish to ask?

• Don't forget to make a note of the judge's summing up.

CASE STUDY

The court usher calls the case number. 'Plaint number 123. Swift versus Knavish & Company (a firm).'

Bill states his case
On the way to the witness box Bill Swift feels his legs turn to jelly and he falters. He shuffles his papers nervously as the usher approaches and asks Bill his religion.

'Church of England,' mumbles Bill.

'Take the Bible in your right hand and read the words on the card.' While he speaks the usher hands Bill a small white card, upon which is written the oath.

Sensing all eyes in the court are turned in his direction, Bill is aware of a cold damp sensation in his palms. Taking two very deep breaths, be avows to tell the truth. He is then asked to identify himself, and in a calm, lucid voice pronounces: 'Bill Swift, hire shop proprietor of 16 Old Town Street, Any Town.' He is now requested to state his claim.

'I am claiming the sum of £2,432.16p for items of equipment hired, namely a small mechanical digger and a cement mixer on the dates as stated on the two invoices, which I submit as evidence numbered one and two.'

Attached to each invoice is a copy of the appropriate hire agreement signed by Ted Knavish. The judge requires to see these documents, so Bill hands them to the usher, who in turn passes them to the judge, who indicates that Bill should continue.

'I personally telephoned Mr Knavish on numerous occasions and wrote many times demanding payment of the outstanding account.'

As he speaks, Bill hands the usher copies of all the letters he has sent to Knavish & Company, together with a copy of a contact form upon which he had written the times, dates and brief notes of their telephone conversations. He also passes to the judge, via the usher, a copy of the customer's sales ledger account. The judge now asks Bill if the defendant told him why he did not pay the account.

'Yes, sir. He told me the equipment arrived late and the cement mixer had broken down. But not until after he had repaired it.'

'What did you do next?' enquires the judge.

'Told him,' pointing to Ted Knavish, 'it wasn't my fault the equipment arrived late.'

'Why was the equipment late, Mr Swift?' enquires the judge.

'I was told by George that the previous hirer of the equipment returned it to my premises late.'

'Who's George? And is he in the court, Mr Swift?'

'George is my mechanic, he checks all the equipment in and out, services and repairs them as required. He will be giving evidence later, sir.'

Throughout Bill's statement the judge questions him on any items he is not clear about. Throughout this time any evidence Bill refers to is passed to the judge, who makes notes. After concluding his claim Bill returns to his seat, and George is called into the witness box, where he repeats the initial procedure.

He tells the judge the normal routine he generally follows when the equipment is hired out and returned. Lifting his head, the judge looks towards George and asks: 'Was this the routine you used on the day the cement mixer and digger were hired to Knavish & Co?'

'No, sir. The cement mixer was due to be returned the previous afternoon. It did not arrive at the yard until the next morning. Mr Swift became very angry at the delay because it was due at Mr Knavish's site at 8.30 that morning. Because it was late I did not have time to inspect the cement mixer.'

'Did you inform Mr Swift?'

'No, sir,' replied George.

Looking thoughtful, the judge makes a further note. Before either Bill or George step down from the witness box, Ted Knavish is invited to put any questions he wishes to ask to them.

Ted Knavish tells his side of the story
The usher invites Ted to enter the other witness box. Swearing an oath and identifying himself, he proceeds to put forward his argument.

'Sir. I called into Mr Swift's hire shop to hire a cement mixer and digger. I gave the time and address of where the items were to be delivered. I needed them to re-turf a small lawn and lay a new drive. Instead of delivering the items at 8.30, they arrive just before lunch. Not only did my son and I lose a morning's work, we were not ready when the sand and cement arrived.'

The judge makes notes and asks questions throughout Ted Knavish's statement. He continued to explain that the driver delivering the sand and cement left it on the road. Unfortunately the driver tipped his load across the drive of the adjoining property. The occupier, a self employed accountant, could neither get in nor out of his drive. So he sent Ted Knavish an invoice for the fees lost. The equipment had been rented for two days. Ted Knavish informs the judge that the cement mixer broke down soon after he and his son started working.

'Sir, I admit I owe Mr Swift some of the money he claims. I tried to offer him what I think I owe after deducting the amounts I was forced to pay out due to his negligence.'

'How much have you requested to be deducted, Mr Knavish?'

'£465.86p, sir. £261.36p for parts and labour required to mend the mixer. I paid my son half a day's wages, which came of £32.50p for doing nothing. The accountant charged me £140.00p for the fees he claimed he had lost. Therefore I am counterclaiming the sum stated, which I asked Mr Swift to deduct from his invoice. But he refused.'

Bill is invited to question any part of Ted Knavish's evidence that he did not agree with or could not understand, before the defendant's expert witness takes the stand.

Shown a copy of the statement he had made earlier, the witness is asked to confirm its accuracy. This he does by confirming that the parts used and the labour costs claimed were correct. He also states these were necessary to return the mixer to its full working order and to meet the requisite safety regulations. Bill is offered a chance to interrogate the witness, but declines.

The judge, confirming that those present had no further questions or anything else to add to their statements, dismisses the witness.

The judge sums up and gives judgement

After reading his notes and deliberating on the testimonies of the plaintiff and defendant the judge gives his reasoning for the judgement he is about to impart.

Looking at Bill Swift, he tells him it was his responsibility to ensure that the equipment he told Mr Knavish he could hire was available at the time promised. Furthermore, the equipment must be suitable and capable of carrying out the task it was manufactured to perform.

Next the judge addresses Ted Knavish, explaining to him that Bill Swift cannot be responsible or accountable for the sand and cement being tipped across a neighbour's drive. It was he, Mr Knavish and his son, who were in attendance on the site; it was their responsibility to supervise where the sand and cement were placed.

Addressing both the plaintiff and the defendant the judge adds that he proposes to award judgement in favour of Mr Swift, in the sum of £2,076.30p. This took into account the sum spent by Mr Knavish to repair the cement mixer, and for the loss of earnings for his son caused by Bill's neglect but discounted part of the counterclaim relating to the accountant's loss of fees. Reduced costs are also awarded to Bill Swift in line with the judgement award. The judge also states when and where these are to be paid. Usually the plaintiff and defendant are asked to confirm the payment details. In this case it is mutually agreed that 28 days from the date of the hearing is a reasonable time. Both Bill Swift and Ted Knavish will be notified of the judgement by the court in the manner previously described.

During the summing up the judge could have pointed out to Ted Knavish that he too could have counterclaimed for loss of earnings.

Please note
This illustration of a court hearing in this case study is fictional.
Whilst based on actual experience, no real cases have been cited and
the judgement is assumed.

DISCUSSION POINTS

1. Do you already use a form suitable for noting main points of
   your conversation when you telephone a customer requesting
   payment?

2. What things could you do to obtain an 'out of court' settlement?

8
Enforcing Judgement

IF YOUR DEBTOR DOES NOT PAY

The mandatory 28 days ordered by the judge have lapsed. You have not been informed by the court that your customer has paid as instructed. The time has now arrived for you to decide on the system of enforcement you want to deploy in order to obtain payment. A number of methods are at your disposal to assist you to reach a decision; the pre-sue report you obtained will be an asset, and will help point you towards the best way to enforce payment.

Executing the judgement
You must let the full 28 days elapse before taking any action to enforce the judgement order. To execute the judge's award you can use either:

- the county court bailiff or
- a high court sheriff.

Bailiff or Sheriff
Whenever possible most litigators tend to use the high court sheriff. He won't go galloping up to your debtor's door with six guns blazing, nor will he come riding out of Nottingham Castle chasing Robin Hood. The reasoning behind this strategy is simple. The county court bailiff is a paid civil servant. There is a possibly unfounded feeling that he has very little or no incentive to collect the judgement debt or to seize goods. The high court sheriff on the other hand, is paid on a commission basis, receiving a percentage of the sum collected or from the proceeds of sale, if goods have been seized.

Amounts which govern your choice
The controlling factor covering which court office to use, for example either bailiff or sheriff, is the amount of the judgement

debt. This can fall into one of three categories:

1. If the award is up to £2,000 a county court bailiff must be used.

2. For awards in excess of £5,000, it is the high court sheriff who must be used to enforce payment of the judgement debt.

3. For judgement sums between £2–5,000, you may use either official.

ISSUING A WARRANT OF EXECUTION

Always bear in mind the following action will only be successful if your defendant has either the money or assets to cover the amount you are owed.

Using a county court bailiff

You will be required to complete form N323 (see Figure 11) to request a 'Warrant of execution' to be issued in the county court. This form can be either taken or posted to the court with the relevant fee. Don't forget the stamped, self addressed envelope if you are applying by post, should you require confirmation of issue.

Notifying the defendant

First your defendant will be informed that the warrant has been issued. He or she will be given only seven days in which to pay the full amount due under the order. If payment is not received in that time a bailiff will call at the address given by you. The bailiff is not able to force entry into the premises of the debtor, but once entry has been gained he cannot be refused re-entry into the premises.

WHAT THE BAILIFF WILL DO

Hopefully he will collect the full sum owing – they make every effort to collect cash. If they fail to receive payment they will levy distress: that is to say they will slap labels on some or all of the debtors' assets sufficient to cover the full judgement debt, and costs of removal and sale of all goods seized. This has the same effect as literally seizing and removing away the goods to be sold at a later date. Later the bailiff will return with ample transport to actually take the chattels away. Items which a bailiff cannot levy against include things like:

Request for Warrant of Execution

To be completed and signed by the plaintiff or his solicitor and sent to the court with the appropriate fee

1 Plaintiff's name and address	WILLIAM SWIFT T/A SWIFT HIRE SHOP 16, OLD TOWN ST ANY TOWN 2X2 2X2	In the	ANY TOWN County Court

Case Number 123

2 Name and address for service and payment (if different from above) Ref/Tel No.

Warrant no.

Issue date:

Warrant applied for at   o'clock

3 Defendant's name and address

EDWARD KNAVISH T/A KNAVISH & Co NEW TOWN ST ANY TOWN 2X1 1X2

Foreign court code/name:

I certify that the whole or part of any instalments due under the judgment or order have not been paid and the balance now due is as shown

4 Warrant details

	£	p
(A) Balance due at date of this request	2413	00
(B) Amount for which warrant to issue	2413	00
Issue fee	50	00
Solicitor's costs		
Land Registry fee		
TOTAL	£ 2463	00

If the amount of the warrant at (B) is less than the balance at (A), the sum due after the warrant is paid will be

Signed *W. Swift*

Plaintiff (Plaintiff's solicitor)

Dated 20/1/9X

IMPORTANT
You must inform the court immediately of any payments you receive after you have sent this request to the court

Other information that might assist the bailiff including the name(s) and address(es) of any 2nd/3rd defendant and other address(es) at which the defendant might have goods. You should also tell the court if you have reason to believe that the bailiff might encounter serious difficulties in attempting to execute the warrant.

Warrant No.

Fig. 11. Request for a warrant of execution (N323).
(Reproduced with permission of HMSO.)

- items belong to the debtor's spouse, unless he or she was named in the summons

- furniture and equipment on hire, leased or subject to a hire purchase agreement

- any article, such as tools, your defendant requires for their job or business

- basic household objects such as bedding, clothing and cooking utensils.

Walking possession agreement

Another option available to the bailiff is to enter into a 'Walking Possession Agreement' with the debtor. This arrangement allows the debtor time to raise the money to pay the judgement and total costs in full. It could be that your debtor is expecting a large cheque in a few days' time from one of his customers. Whenever possible the bailiff will do his utmost to obtain a cash settlement. Not until he has exhausted this process will goods normally be removed.

Application to suspend a warrant of execution

Your defendant can apply to the court to suspend your warrant at any time by using form N245 (Figure 12). The court will send you a copy of their application together with their reasons. Normally it is because they now wish to make an offer to pay by instalments. You will reply to the offer as described in Chapter 4. The requisite form for accepting or declining your defendant's request will be enclosed with the copy of the defendant's application.

Reissuing a suspended warrant

If a warrant of execution is suspended for any reason, it can be reinstated on the following grounds:

- you agreed to your defendant's offer to pay, but he did not

- the debtor moved away from the address stated on the warrant, and you have located his new address

- your debtor's circumstances changed, and he can now afford to pay.

To reissue a warrant requires you to submit to the court form N445 (see Figure 13). A warrant of execution can be reissued up to twelve months from the original date of the warrant free of charge. When a

Fig. 12. Application to suspend a warrant (N245).
(Reproduced with permission of HMSO.)

6 Income

My usual take home pay *including overtime, commission, bonuses etc.*	£	per
Income support	£	per
Child benefit(s)	£	per
Other state benefit(s)	£	per
My pension(s)	£	per
Others living in my home give me	£	per
Other income *(give details below)*		
	£	per
	£	per
	£	per
Total income	£	per

8 Priority debts

(This section is for arrears only. Do not include regular expenses listed in box 7.)

Rent arrears		£	per
Mortgage arrears		£	per
Community charge arrears		£	per
Water charge arrears		£	per
Fuel debts:	Gas	£	per
	Electricity	£	per
	Other	£	per
Maintenance arrears		£	per
Others *(give details below)*			
		£	per
		£	per
Total priority debts		£	per

7 Expenses

(Do not include any payments made by other members of the household out of their own income)

I have regular expenses as follows:

Mortgage *(including second mortgage)*	£	per
Rent	£	per
Community charge	£	per
Gas	£	per
Electricity	£	per
Water charges	£	per
TV rental and licence	£	per
HP repayments	£	per
Mail order	£	per
Housekeeping, food, school meals	£	per
Travelling expenses	£	per
Children's clothing	£	per
Maintenance payments	£	per
Others *(not court orders or credit debts listed in boxes 9 and 10)*		
	£	per
	£	per
	£	per
Total expenses	£	per

9 Court orders

Court	Case No.	£	per
Total court order instalments		£	per

Of the payments above, I am behind with payments to *(please list)*

10 Credit debts

Loans and credit card debts *(please list)*

	£	per
	£	per
	£	per

Of the payments above, I am behind with payments to *(please list)*

11 Offer of Payment

• *If you take away the totals of boxes 7, 8 and 9 and the payments you are making in box 10 from the total in box 6, you will get some idea of the sort of sum you should offer. The offer you make should be one you can afford.*

I can pay £ _____ a month

(and I enclose £ _____)

12 Declaration

I declare that the details I have given above are true to the best of my knowledge

Signed _____   Dated _____

Fig. 12. (continued).

Request for Reissue of Warrant

Tick appropriate box and enter case number and warrant number

In the

ANY TOWN **County Court**

Case Number 123

Warrant Number 456

Type of warrant		
✓	Warrant of execution	
☐	Warrant of possession	
☐	Warrant of delivery	
☐	Warrant of committal	

1 Plaintiff's name

WILLIAM SWIFT

2 Name and address for service and payment

WILLIAM SWIFT
16, OLD TOWN ST.
ANY TOWN

Ref/Tel No. 2×2 2×2

3 Defendant's name and address

EDWARD KNAVISH
T/A KNAVISH & CO
NEW TOWN ST
ANY TOWN

2×1 1×2

I certify that the whole or part of any instalments due under the judgment or order have not been paid and the balance now due is as shown (* and that the amount due under the part warrant is as shown at (B))

4 Warrant details

(A) Balance of judgment or order due at date of this request including fee and costs of warrant issue.

£2463·00

Signed *W. Swift*

Plaintiff (Plaintiff's solicitor)

Dated 15/3/9x

* delete if not a part warrant

(B) **Parts warrants only**
Balance due under the warrant (including the fee and costs of warrant issue)

If the amount of the warrant at (B) is less than the balance at (A), the sum due after the warrant is paid will be

IMPORTANT
You must inform the court immediately of any payments you receive after you have sent this request to the court

Reasons for requesting reissue (information you are relying on to support your application for reissue eg address for execution has changed, failure to make payments under a suspended order etc. You should also tell the court if you have reason to believe that the bailiff might encounter any serious difficulty in attempting to execute the warrant.)

DEFENDANT FAILED TO MAKE REPAYMENTS
OF £100 PER MONTH UNDER THE SUSPENDED ORDER

Reissue No.

Fig. 13. Request to reissue a warrant (N445).
(Reproduced with permission of HMSO.)

bailiff is told the defendant have moved away, but you know this is untrue, supply the bailiff with a description or photograph of the defendant with form N445.

Objecting to a warrant's suspension
If you disagree with the suspension of your debtor's warrant, or the amount they are now offering to pay, a hearing will be granted by the court and your objection will be considered alongside the defendant's application. The procedures are as those explained in the earlier chapters.

Proceeds of sale
When a bailiff has seized goods from a debtor, they are sold by auction. The proceeds of the sale, less the sale expenses which would include auctioneer's commission, transport and labour costs, are handed into the court. All monies paid to the court, including any sums paid voluntarily or collected by the bailiff, will be held by the court for 14 days. After this time the court will release all the money it holds to you, the plaintiff.

DEFINING COURT REPORTS

In due course, after executing the warrant of execution, the bailiff will report back to you, usually within one month from the date of the warrant. Hopefully the bailiff will have collected the full debt in cash, if not he will advise you of his actions.

What the reports will say
Standard wordings in the reports from the bailiff following the issue of a warrant of execution are summarised below.

Gone away – unable to trace
This means exactly what is says. Since issuing the summons and obtaining judgement your defendant changed his address. Perhaps you instructed the bailiff incorrectly. The bailiff will not trace your debtor for you, it is up to you to do this. But once you have located the defendant's new residence (a good debt collecting agency will do this for you for a reasonable fee), you can reissue the warrant by using form N445 (Figure 13).

No assets upon which to restrain
This tells you either the debtor's belongings have no value or they

are subject to finance agreements. Check your pre-sue report: if it lists any unencumbered assets send a copy of the report to the bailiff when you reissue the 'Warrant of execution'. No fees are charged for reissue, remember.

Unable to gain entry
Either your debtor was out when the bailiff called, or he refused to let him enter the premises. A county court bailiff has no powers to force an entry to the debtor's premises, he must be invited in. But once entry is gained, he cannot be refused re-entry.

He has a walking possession agreement with the debtor
This confirms that the bailiff gained entry to your defendant's property, took an inventory of all saleable assets, which the debtor has agreed and has signed a document stating he will not remove or sell any of those items listed. This arrangement also stops any other bailiff from taking the goods against another judgement order. If the bailiff discovers the debtor is not complying with the agreement, for example he did not comply with his offer to pay, the bailiff is empowered to remove the goods listed and sell them. Sales of all repossessed chattels are sold at auction, this being the most expedient method of disposal.

CHANGING COURTS

In order to make use of the high court sheriff, you must first transfer your judgement order from the lower court. Transferring your case between courts does not involve you in any further hearings, and the procedure is easy.

Instructing a high court sheriff
Assuming your debt is of a size where you have the option to use either a bailiff or sheriff, it is recommended that you use the sheriff. To do this you must now transfer your case and judgement to the high court. This means you will need to obtain from the county court a 'special certificate of judgement'. The simple steps required to obtain this certificate are explained below.

'Praecipe' for a 'Writ of Fieri Facias'
Commonly known as 'Fi Fa', samples of these forms E1 and F1 are shown in Figures 14 and 15. You take the completed 'Praecipe' along to the county court, which will endorse the 'Writ of Fi Fa' and

issue a special certificate of judgement. You now take both of these documents to the local office of the under sheriff, with a small fee. The rest of the endorsement can be safely left in the hands of the high court sheriff. He will execute the warrant in the same manner as would the county court bailiff.

Acting without a solicitor
You do not need to employ a solicitor to transfer the judgement between the two courts. However, if you want your claim dealt with in the high court from the outset, you would have no option but to employ a lawyer. So you can see it is more expedient to issue a summons in the county court, which you can undertake yourself, then transfer judgement to the high court for enforcement.

No choice
It may be the nature of your case justifies it being heard in the high court leaving you without choice. Only you can decide if the amount of the claim is worth the extra risk and additional costs. A pre-sue search will establish if your debtor has the ability to satisfy a judgement debt before proceeding – assuming you are fortunate enough to win your case. Prior to committing yourself to this extra expense you can seek an appraisal of your case. It is only those actions for substantial sums and which encompass lengthy legal argument which may set precedents which will warrant these extra costs. The district judge will advise you on those points of law affecting you.

QUESTIONS AND ANSWERS

How long does it take to issue a warrant of execution?

About 14 days. First the defendant is notified the warrant has been issued and they are given only seven days to pay the amount owed in full.

Who pays the bailiff's costs?

You do to issue the warrant. The bailiff will add this sum to the existing judgement debt and costs, and the defendant will reimburse you.

What if the goods fetch more than the judgement debt?

Any cash left after the debt and all costs have been paid the surplus is returned to the defendant.

IN THE HIGH COURT OF JUSTICE

Division

District Registry

Between   19 .— .—No.

WILLIAM SWIFT

Plaintiff

AND

EDWARD KNAVISH

Defendant

Seal a Writ of Fieri Facias directed to the Sheriff of

against EDWARD KNAVISH

of NEW TOWN ST, ANY TOWN

in the County of COUNTY

(1) Or "Order" or "Award".

upon a Judgment (¹)   dated the 3 RD

day of DECEMBER, 199X, for the sum of £ 2367.16

debt and £ 80.84 costs and interest, etc.

Indorsed to levy £ 2463.00 and interest thereon at £10·00 per

centum per annum, from the 26 TH day of OCTOBER

(2) Add additional words or certificate under Exchange Control Act 1947, if applicable.

199X, and £ 50.00 costs of execution. (²)

(Solicitors Name)
(Address)   N/A
Agent for
of

W. Swift (PLAINTIFF)   Solicitor   for the

Fig. 14. Praecipe (E1).
Reproduced with permission of HMSO).

Writ of
Fieri Facias
(O. 45, r. 12)

IN THE HIGH COURT OF JUSTICE   19   .—   .—High Court No.

Division   County Court Plaint No. 123

[(On transfer from   ANY TOWN   County Court)]

Between

WILLIAM SWIFT   Plaintiff

AND

EDWARD KNAVISH   Defendant

ELIZABETH THE SECOND, by the Grace of God, of the United Kingdom of Great Britain, Northern Ireland and of Our other realms and territories Queen, Head of the Commonwealth, Defender of the Faith.

To the sheriff of   ANY TOWN   greeting:

(1) "adjudged" or "ordered"

Whereas in the above-named action it was on the   day of
, 19   . (1). ORDERED   in this Court [or in the
ANY TOWN   County Court under plaint No.   ]

(2) Name of Defendant.

(3) Name of Plaintiff.

that the Defendant (2)   EDWARD KNAVISH
do pay the Plaintiff (3)   WILLIAM SWIFT
£ 2367.16   [and £ 84.84   [costs] [costs to be taxed, which
costs have been taxed and allowed at £   as appears by the
certificate of the taxing officer dated the   day of
19   ]]:

WE COMMAND YOU that of the goods, chattels and other property of (2)
EDWARD KNAVISH

(4) The words in this set of square brackets are to be omitted where the judgment or order is for less than £600 and does not entitle the Plaintiff to costs against whom the writ is issued.

(5) Insert the appropriate rate of interest at date of entry of judgment.

(6) "judgment" or "order"

in your county authorised by law to be seized in execution you cause to be made
the sum[s] of £ 2367.16   (4) [and £ 80.84   for costs of
execution] and also interest on £ 2448.00   at the rate of (5) £ 10
per cent per annum from the   26TH   day of OCTOBER , 194X,
until payment (4) [together with sheriff's poundage, officers' fees, costs of levying
and all other legal, incidental expenses] and that immediately after execution of this
writ you pay (3)   WILLIAM SWIFT

in pursuance of the said (6)   ORDER   the amount levied in respect of
the said sum and interest.

AND WE ALSO COMMAND YOU that you indorse on this writ immediately after execution thereof a statement of the manner in which you have executed it and send a copy of the statement to (3)

Witness

Lord High Chancellor of Great Britain.

the   day of   19

Fig. 15. Writ of 'Fi Fa' (F1).
(Reproduced with permission of HMSO.)

Why does the court take 14 days to release any money it holds?

Because if insolvency proceedings have been originated against the debtor by another creditor the court will suspend your action. Any funds it may hold must be handed to the appointed Official Receiver or insolvency practitioner.

What happens to these funds?

The funds are held to the order of all creditors of the insolvent estates, and will now be distributed in the correct order of priority.

How would the warrant be served in respect of a partnership?

You will be required to instruct the bailiff to execute the warrant at each of the debtor's addresses, for which additional fees would need to be paid. If you are canny use the pre-sue search, and instruct the bailiff to attend the address of the partner with the greater number of valuable assets upon which to levy.

Will the sheriff's reports be the same as the bailiff's?

Yes. The main difference between the two is their employment contracts. Being self employed the sheriff may bill you for travelling expenses on abortive visits to the defendant's property.

CHECKLIST

- Establish that 28 clear days have elapsed since obtaining judgement.
- Confirm the total amount of debt and costs.
- Choose between using a bailiff or sheriff.
- Issue your warrant of execution.
- Complete the *praecipe* to change courts.
- Have the Writ of Fi Fa endorsed.

CASE STUDIES

Bill instructs the county court bailiff

Feeling that the problem of transferring judgement to the high court for enforcement is beyond his capability, Bill Swift goes to his local county court to collect the form N323, which he completes and returns to the court with the appropriate fee. After receiving notice of service, he waits for the bailiff's report. When he is informed that the bailiff agreed to a walking possession agreement with Ted Knavish, he feels his action is at last beginning to pay off. Three weeks later he receives payment of all the money owed by his customer together with interest and costs.

Karen goes to the high court

Thinking the high court sheriff has more incentive to enforce the judgement order she was awarded, Karen obtains forms E1 and F1, filling in the *Praecipe* for a Writ of *Fieri Facias*. At her county court she hands over the documents with her fee, and it is endorsed. Sending the writ together with the special certificate of judgement to the local under sheriff, with another small fee, she is now content to leave the matter safely in the sheriff's capable hands. Karen returns to her office confident in the knowledge that not only can she issue a summons but also she is able to obtain and enforce a judgement order, including transferring the claim to the high court, without using a solicitor.

Ted makes a promise

When the bailiff calls, Ted Knavish wishing to discharge his obligations, lets him enter his property. It was shortage of cash which got him into this mess. It was never his intention not to pay the money owed. He comes to an agreement with the bailiff, who makes an inventory of Ted's saleable assets after he has agreed to pay the sum due from the proceeds of a cheque he is expecting in ten days' time. The last thing Ted Knavish wants to see is his furniture taken away and sold. It rarely fetches its true value at auction. When the cheque Ted was expecting arrives he goes along to the court with a copy of the warrant of execution and settles the full amount of the outstanding judgement and costs.

DISCUSSION POINTS

1. Would it be worth your while to use a high court sheriff?

2. Would you be squeamish about having your debtor's possessions seized?

9
Other Options for Enforcement

ALTERNATIVE METHODS OF PAYMENT

Usually the most common method used for enforcing payment on a judgement order is the 'Warrant of execution', as explained in the previous chapter. But for some debtors an alternative means of enforcement could be better. To find out if the other options are suitable for your own debtor, let's look at what is available.

Looking at your preferences

Apart from issuing a 'Warrant of execution' and instructing a bailiff, or moving judgement to the high court and using a sheriff, there are other means of enforcing payment of the judgement awarded which are equally effective.

ATTACHMENT OF EARNINGS ORDER

This means of enforcement can only be used if your debtor is employed. Because you have judgement on a trade debt doesn't mean you cannot use this method. Since you issued a summons perhaps your customer stopped trading and found himself employment. Being a sole trader he will find himself still responsible and personally liable for all the outstanding business debts. It is up to you to find out if your debtor is in work, the court will not do this for you. There are four things you can do to establish if your debtor is working:

1. Search the attachment of earnings register at his local county court; this will tell you:
   (a) if your customer has other attachment of earnings orders registered
   (b) whether they are employed
   (c) details of their employer.

2. Telephone your debtor's business address; this will confirm if they are still in business. If not you can make your own enquiries locally.

3. If your pre-sue search gave no indication of employment, re-instruct your debt collection or credit reference agency.

4. Ask for an oral examination (see below).

Searching the register

To search the attachment of earnings index you must either use form N336 as shown in Figure 16 or write a letter. A small fee is charged by the courts for searching the register. Send either of the above to your debtor's local county court, with a stamped self addressed envelope for their reply.

Consolidating your debt

After searching the attachment of earnings register, and discovering other attachment of earnings orders against your debtor, what can you do? You can make application using the form shown in Figure 5 to ask the court to consolidate your debt with the existing order. This will enable you to obtain an attachment of earnings order without paying another fee. You are not the only one who can request a consolidated order. Your debtor or his employer can also request it at any time. This allows your debtor's employer to make one deduction to cover all orders each pay day, instead of a number of little ones.

Where to apply for an attachment of earnings order

These orders can only be dealt with in the defendant's local court. You must transfer your case if judgement was obtained elsewhere. Simply make an application for transfer using the form in Figure 5, stating your reason for the transfer. In this instance it is because you wish to apply for an attachments of earnings order. Take or send the completed form to the court where judgement was awarded, and they will send the case file to the appropriate court. When the defendant's local court receives the case papers, they will issue you with a new plaint number. It is only this number which can be used when you make future enquiries at the court. It normally takes about 14 days for the court to assemble your papers and pass them to the other court, and for you to be notified of the new case number. This interval can vary depending on how busy the courts are at the time of application.

IN THE ___ANY TOWN___ COUNTY COURT

BETWEEN ....___WILLIAM SWIFT___....................PLAINTIFF

AND ....___EDWARD KNAVISH___.................DEFENDANT

To the Chief Clerk of the ___ANY TOWN___ County Court

Please search your attachment of earnings order index and notify me whether any, and if so what, information is recorded in the name of

___EDWARD KNAVISH___

whose address is

___NEW TOWN ST___
___ANY TOWN   2X1 1X2___

against whom I have obtained a judgement in the ___ANY TOWN COUNTY___ Court, under case number ___123___

DATED

___PLAINTIFF'S___
~~Solicitor~~'s Address

Signed
Plaintiff('s Solicitor)

Solicitor's Ref :—

To the Plaintiff('s Solicitor)

A search of the attachment of earnings order index has been made against the above named defendant and I certify that:—

(1)There are no subsisting entries.

(1) Delete where inapplicable

(1)An attachment of earnings order in respect of a judgement debt is in force in the
County Court. The normal deduction rate
is £   per week/month (1) and the balance outstanding is £

(1)A priority attachment of earnings order in respect of a fine/maintenance order (1)
is in force in the   Court.

DATED

Chief Clerk

N.336 Request for and result of search in the attachment of earnings index
Order 27 Rule 2(3)

Fig. 16. Request to search the attachment of earnings index (N336).
(Reproduced with permission of HMSO.)

Making your application
You will need form N337 (see Figure 17). This is sent to the defendant's local court with a fee, the amount of which depends on the amount you are claiming and will be added to the order. It is recommended that an additional fee be paid to have a bailiff serve your petition personally upon the defendant. This helps to reduce the time factor. You will not be required to attend court to procure an attachments of earnings order. It is only if you disagree with the order when made that a hearing will be called.

Statement of means
Your defendant will receive a notice from the court asking him or her to pay the outstanding debt or, failing that, to complete a form similar to form N9A (Figure 8). In this form, referred to as a 'Statement of Means', your debtor must provide information about his employment, earnings and supply details of all outgoings.

Assessing the amount of the order
A district judge will decide how much the defendant can afford to pay. This will be determined after deducting from your defendant's net income the protected earning rate. This is the sum the court allows for:

- food
- rent or mortgage interest
- council tax
- essential clothing.

The amount of the order will be forward to your debtor's employers, telling them how much to deduct from the defendant's wages, how often and where it is to be remitted.

Objecting to an attachment of earnings order
You will receive a copy of the attachment of earnings order. If you object to the amount of the order made, because you have evidence that your defendant is earning more than he stated on his form, you can make an application using form N244 (Figure 5) to request the district judge to reconsider what is a fair amount to pay, by submitting copies of your proof. Your pre-sue search will be a good guide.

Reissue of post judgement proceedings
Once the court makes an order against your defendant for specific

Request for Attachment of Earnings Order

To be completed and signed by the plaintiff or his solicitor and sent to the court with the appropriate fee

1 Plaintiff's name and address

WILLIAM SWIFT
T/A SWIFTS HIRE SHOP
16 OLD TOWN ST
ANY TOWN   2X2 2X2

In the

ANY TOWN   County Court

Case Number   123

2 Name and address for service and payment
(if different from above)
Ref/Tel No.

For court use only

A / E application no.

Issue date:

Hearing date:

3 Defendant's name and address

EDWARD KNAVISH
NEW TOWN ST
ANY TOWN
2X1 1X2

on

at   o'clock

at (address)

4 Judgment details

Court where judgment/order made if not court of issue

I apply for an attachment of earnings order

5 Outstanding debt

Balance due at date of this request*
(excluding issue fee but including unsatisfied warrant costs)

*you may also be entitled to interest to date of request where judgment is for over £5000 and is entered on or after 1 July 1991

Balance due	2463	00
Issue fee	70	00
AMOUNT NOW DUE	2533	00

I certify that the whole or part of any instalments due under the judgment or order have not been paid and the balance now due is as shown

Signed *W. Swift*

Plaintiff (Plaintiff's solicitor)

Dated 15/4/9X

6 Employment Details (please give as much information as you can - it will help the court to make an order more quickly)

Employer's name and address

THE GARDEN CENTRE
FLOWER ST
ANY TOWN
2X3 3X2

Defendant's place of work
(if different from employer's address)

The defendant is employed as   HEAD GARDNER

Works No / Pay Ref

7 Other details
(Give any other details about the defendant's circumstances which may be relevant to the application)

IMPORTANT
You must inform the court immediately of any payments you receive after you have sent this request to the court

Fig. 17. Request for an attachment of earnings order (N337).
(Reproduced with permission of HMSO.)

sums to be paid either in a lump or at regular intervals, your action is automatically suspended. If your debtor does not pay as ordered, you can, by using form N446 (see Figure 18), request the defendant be brought before the court to be examined orally. This is also a request for the reissue of post judgement proceedings. You can also use form N446 if your debtor changes jobs and you wish to transfer the attachment of earnings order to their new employer.

Regular payments
Once an attachment of earnings order has been made you will receive regular payments from the court or direct from your debtor's place of work, depending upon the order made by the court. It is now up to you to contact the court if any irregularities occur in the debtor's payment rhythm. Simply ask the clerk at the court to check why payments are not being made as ordered. The most common reason for non-payment is due to your defendant becoming unemployed or changing his job.

ORAL EXAMINATIONS

This is not a method for enforcing judgement. An oral examination allows you to question your debtor about his financial position. Should your defendant be a limited company, you can question a director about the company's fiscal standing. Your pre-sue search will give you the information you require. But if it has been some time since you obtained the original pre-sue report, it can be cheaper to request an oral examination than to commission a new report. Although using an oral examination takes a little longer, it can be used to obtain information about hidden assets. To request an oral examination you must use either form N316 (see Figure 19) or N446 (see above). Send your completed document to the court with the required fee, plus a stamped addressed envelope and an additional sum to cover personal service by a bailiff. Both the defendant and yourself will be notified of the time and the date of the review. The hearing will be carried out in chambers.

Attending an oral examination
The examination will be conducted in private. The only people present will be the defendant, the district judge and yourself. The defendant will be on oath to tell the truth; you can only ask questions about his financial status, so be prepared and make a list of all the questions you want to ask, such as:

Request for Reissue of Enforcement or Oral Examination (not warrant)

In the **ANY TOWN** County Court

Case Number **123**

Type of process			
Tick appropriate box and enter case number and number of process	✓	Attachment of earnings	A/E No. **789**
		Oral examination	O/E No.
		Judgment summons	J/S No.
		Other *(state ward, charging order, garnishee etc.)*	No.

1 Plaintiff's name: WILLIAM SWIFT

2 Name and address for service and payment: 16, OLD TOWN ST ANY TOWN

Ref/Tel No. 2×2 2×2

3 Defendant's name and address: EDWARD KNAVISH NEW TOWN ST ANY TOWN

2×1 1×2

4 Outstanding debt

A) Balance due* at date of this request (including costs of issue of post-judgment process, and unsatisfied warrant costs*)
*including any interest to date of request where judgment is over £5000 and entered on or after 1 July 1991
*except where reissuing oral examination

2,300.00 ◄

Unsatisfied warrant costs (oral examinations only)

B) Judgment summonses only
Amount due under the judgment summons (do not include amounts for which defendant imprisoned)

IMPORTANT
You must inform the court immediately of any payments you receive after you have sent this request to the court

---

For court use only

Hearing Date:

at   o'clock

at *(address)*

Reissue date:

I certify that (*the whole or part of any instalments due under the judgment or order have not been paid and that) the balance now due under this judgment is as shown (†and that the amount due under the judgment summons is as shown at (B))

Signed *W. Swift*

Plaintiff (Plaintiff's solicitor)

Dated **23/7/9X**

* delete if you are applying to reissue an oral examination
† delete if not applying to reissue judgment summons

Reasons for requesting reissue (*information you are relying on to support your application for reissue eg defendant address (or employment) has changed, he has failed to make payments under a suspended order etc.*)

Reissue No.

N446 ...

Fig. 18. Request for reissue of enforcement (N446).
(Reproduced with permission of HMSO.)

Request for Oral Examination

to be completed and signed by the plaintiff or his solicitor and sent to the court with the appropriate fee

1 Plaintiff's name and address

WILLIAM SWIFT
16 OLD TOWN ST
ANY TOWN
2X2 2X2

In the

ANY TOWN   County Court

Case Number 123

2 Name and address for service and payment
(if different from above)
Ref/Tel No.

For court use only

O/E no.

Issue date:

3 Defendant's name and address

EDWARD KNAVISH
NEW TOWN ST
ANY TOWN
2X1 1X2

Hearing date:

on

at   o'clock

at (address)

4 Name and address of person to be orally examined if different from Box 3

(ie director of defendant company)

5 Judgment details

Court where judgment/order made if not court of issue

I apply for an order that the above defendant (the officer of the defendant company named in Box 4) attend and be orally examined as to his (the defendant company's) financial circumstances and produce at the examination any relevant books or documents

6 Outstanding debt

you may be able to claim interest if judgment entered for more than £5000 on or after 1 July 1991

Balance of debt and any interest*/damages at date of this request	2330	00
Issue fee	20	00
AMOUNT NOW DUE	2150	00
Unsatisfied warrant costs		

I certify that the balance now due is as shown

Signed *W. Swift*
                                    Plaintiff (Plaintiff's solicitor)

Dated 15/8/9X

IMPORTANT
You must inform the court immediately of any payments you
receive after you have sent this request to the court

Fig. 19. Request for an oral examination (N316).
(Reproduced with permission of HMSO.)

Affidavit in support of Application for Garnishee Order Absolute

Plaintiff	WILLIAM SWIFT
Defendant	EDWARD KNAVISH
Garnishee	ANY TOWN BANK

HIGH ST

ANY TOWN

2×5 5×2

In the

ANY TOWN County Court

Case No. *always quote this* 123

Plaintiff's Ref.

Seal

(¹)Insert full name address and occupation of deponent

I,(1) WILLIAM SWIFT, PROPRIETOR SWIFT HIRE SHOP 16, OLD TOWN ST, ANY TOWN

(Solicitor for) the above-named plaintiff, make oath and say:

1. That I (or
   on the 3RD day DECEMBER 199X , obtained a judgment (or an order) in this court against the above-named defendant for payment of the sum of £ 2463·00 for debt (or damages) and costs

(²)where judgment entered for more than £5000 on or after 1 July 1991

2. That £ 2300·00 , including any interest to date(2), is still due and unpaid under the judgment (order).

3. That to the best of my information or belief the garnishee, ANY TOWN BANK
   of HIGH ST, ANY TOWN 2×5 5×2

(³)add if known

is indebted to the defendant (in the sum of £ 2300·00)(3)

(⁴)state your grounds

The reasons for my information or belief are:(4)
AN ORAL EXAMINATION HELD AT ANY TOWN COUNTY COURT ON 23/8/9X

4. That the garnishee is a deposit-taking institution having more than one place of business (and the name and address of the branch at which the defendant's account is believed to be held is:

(⁵)delete as appropriate

and the number of the account is believed to be) (I do not know at which branch the defendant's account is held, or what the number of the account is)(5)

5. That the last known address of the defendant is: NEW TOWN ST ANY TOWN 2×1 1×2

Sworn at	in the
county of	this
day of	19

Before me

This affidavit is filed on behalf of the plaintiff

Officer of a court, appointed by the Circuit Judge to take affidavits

The court office at

Fig. 20. Affidavit supporting a garnishee order (N349).
(Reproduced with permission of HMSO.)

108

- full details of all their current and savings accounts
- where they work and how much they earn
- if the family home is owned or rented
- amount of rent or mortgage, and to whom it is paid
- details of all existing finance agreements, and the total amount paid each month
- investments such as stocks and shares or property.

If you ask any questions not pertinent to establishing his means to pay the judgement order the district judge will intervene and stop you. Knowing the value of your customer's worth can help you decide on the ideal method to enforce payment.

OBTAINING A GARNISHEE ORDER

This order is used to authorise a third party to release any sum of money they are holding on behalf of or to the order of the defendant, and pay this sum to the court to settle the outstanding judgement debt and costs – for instance, money your debtor may have hidden in a building society account.

What you must do
At the oral examination you may have discovered your debtor was owed an amount of money from a third party, and you were previously unaware of its existence. To get at this money you can apply to the court for a garnishee order; to do this you will need:

- notice of issue form (N205A – Figure 7)
- a certificate of judgement
- signed affidavit.

The affidavit using form N349 (Figure 20) must be sworn in front of either an officer of the court or your own solicitor. The court will serve a garnishee order on the third party and a copy to your debtor. The garnishee must now pay the money they hold belonging to your debtor into the court within eight days.

Knowing when to issue a garnishee
Speed and timing are essential elements for successfully issuing a

garnishee. You must know precisely the name and address of the person or firm holding the debtor's money. A garnishee order is only effective against money held by the third party at the time of service of the order. It does not attach to any future monies which are likely to arise.

What the garnishee must do
When a garnishee receives the order, he must pay to the court sufficient monies to discharge the judgement debt and all costs to date. They must not release any monies to the debtor until the order has been satisfied. However, if your debtor removed the money before the order was served the garnishee must inform the court at once. Immediately you are advised of the situation you must ask the court to withdraw the garnishee proceedings. This prevents the debtor claiming costs against you.

UNDERSTANDING A CHARGING ORDER

This method of enforcing your judgement is not recommended, unless you employ a solicitor. It used to be another extremely effective method of getting paid, but is less so in these times of negative equity. But it is something to keep in mind if you are owed a substantial amount of money. If, during the oral examination or in your pre-sue search, it was discovered that your customer, a sole trader, owned a property which was worth more than the amount of mortgage outstanding upon it, you could make application to the court to have a charging order placed upon the property. This action forces the defendant to pay the judgement debt and costs from the proceeds of sale, should he sell the property charged. You cannot, however, make the debtor sell the property:

- until either the first mortgagee takes possession
- or you make application to the court for a forced sale order.

The courts are reluctant to issue an order for sale in respect of a smallish trade debt (besides the costs would not justify such action). Nor are they likely to grant an order if:

- the property is the matrimonial home
- children are living in the property
- your debtor is not in arrears with his first mortgage
- the debtor's spouse is not party to the judgement debt.

In the last point raised, the spouse would be entitled to half of the equity of the property, thus reducing your chances of receiving full repayment of the remaining debt. Unless you know something about property searches or are an expert conveyancer, this course of action should not be tried on your own.

QUESTIONS AND ANSWERS

Can I get an attachment of earnings order against all judgement debtors?

Not all. For example, they must be in paid employment. But if your debtor had joined the armed services or the merchant marine, you would be unable to get an order. There are special arrangements, and in these circumstances you should enquire at your local court.

Are there any disadvantages in consolidating an order?

Yes. It usually means you can expect to receive a smaller amount less frequently than an ordinary attachment of earnings order.

How long does it take to get an attachment of earnings order?

The court usually takes about two weeks after receiving your request to issue an order. It depends on how busy the courts are at the time of the application. It is recommended you pay a small additional fee and have a bailiff serve your debtor with the petition.

Can an attachment of earnings order be suspended?

Yes, the defendant can apply to the court to suspend an attachment of earnings order if he does not want the court to contact his employer. The courts will always allow the suspension if they feel the order would prejudice his employment.

How will I be paid if the court suspends an order?

The court will order the debtor to pay you direct. If he doesn't pay you as ordered you can request the court to lift the suspension.

How long do I have to object to an order?

If you have grounds to object to the attachment of earnings order made by the court, you have 16 days from the date postmarked on the envelope in which the copy of the order arrived. You will be notified in the normal manner when to attend the court for the hearing.

What happens if the garnishee disregards the order?

The garnishee will be responsible for paying the judgement debt. If they are holding funds at the time the order is served the money must be paid into the court.

CHECKLIST

Judgement can be aided by an oral examination and enforced by:

- a warrant of execution
- using a bailiff or sheriff
- an attachment of earnings order
- a garnishee order
- a charging order.

CASE STUDIES

Bill follows a hunch

Not having heard from his customer Ted Knavish since the judgement hearing, Bill Swift calls at his home. Mrs Knavish answers the door, and Bill enquires about Mr Knavish's business. He is told that he is no longer trading, and is working at the local garden centre. Because his debtor ignored the judgement order Bill Swift decides that an attachment of earnings order is the only course he can take to get the money he is owed. Searching the attachment of earnings register at Ted Knavish's local court Bill discovers his ex-customer has another order registered against him, and learns the full name and address of Ted Knavish's employer. After transferring the judgement to his debtor's local court, Bill is awarded an attachment of earnings order on Ted Knavish's income. Bill Swift immediately applies to the court to have the two orders consolidated.

Karen requests an oral examination

Karen makes her way to the judge's chambers on the day of the hearing. She has prepared herself by listing all the question she wants to ask about Ted Knavish's financial standing. Although the examination is heard in chambers, Ted Knavish is still asked to take the oath. The judge explains the procedure to the defendant, and invites Karen to ask her questions. These must relate only to the defendant's assets and income. Any other questions Karen may put will be disallowed. During the examination Karen enquires about the property her debtor lives in: its value, how much is owed on it and the name and address of the mortgage lender and any other charges to the property. She asks about bank and building society accounts, both savings and current. Karen also delves into what motor vehicle he owns and if it is subject to any finance agreements.

The inquisition is relentless, as Karen asks about Ted Knavish's employers, and other court orders. During this process the judge may intervene if she ask the wrong type of questions. He will certainly make his own enquiries of Ted, to help him reach a decision. Throughout this time the defendant is on oath to tell the truth. Because some defendants lie, it is advisable to include questions to which you know the answers, in order to check. Now Karen possesses sufficient information to know the right course of action to take to enforce judgement.

Ted gets a garnishee order placed on his bank account
Receiving notice from the court that a garnishee order had been placed on his bank account, Ted rushes round to the bank and attempts to withdraw all his money before it is paid into the court. He thinks it will be far better for him to flee to Brazil and join Ronnie Biggs than to pay his debts. Fortunately, for the plaintiff, the order must be served on the garnishee before or at the same time as on the defendant; this stops people like Ted Knavish avoiding their liabilities. By the time he arrives at his bank, the account has been frozen.

DISCUSSION POINTS

1. What could be the advantages and disadvantages to you of consolidating an attachment of earnings order?

2. How do you think you would cope with asking the probing financial questions necessary at an oral examination?

3. What methods of enforcement would you be most likely to use?

10
Speeding the Process

TAKING A SHORT CUT

It is not necessary to issue a summons to recover a debt. There is another way, a way that by-passes the small claims and county court system. There are certain tactical advantages to be gained by issuing a notice under section 122(f) of the Insolvency Act 1986. These 'statutory demands' can be served against all classes of debtors, limited companies, partnerships or individuals such as sole traders.

A brief look at the Insolvency Act

To summarise, section 122(f) of the Act permits a company to be wound-up, if it is unable to pay its debts as they become due. You must be able to prove to the court that a company is incapable of paying its debts. To define this proof, look at section 123(e) of the Act. This clearly states 'A company is deemed to be unable to pay its debts as they fall due, by forwarding a final notice to the company's registered office, giving it seven days to pay the account in full'. This will be sufficient proof in court, if the company fails to pay in accordance with the demand. Partnerships and individuals including sole traders can also be dealt with in this manner. To take this route, the debt must not be less than £750. But beware of the pitfalls of using this method of collection, because for this every short cut there is a price tag. Sometimes the price you may end up paying can simply be too much.

Advantages of issuing a statutory demand
The statutory demand can be an extremely useful instrument to use against your debtor. If your customer is happily trading yet is delaying payment of its accounts to improve their own cash flow, they will pay you immediately they receive a statutory demand, for the following reasons:

- they are solvent

- they do not wish to be wound-up
- they are afraid their other suppliers will suspect they are in financial difficulties
- it would upset their bankers.

Disadvantages of taking this path
The main disadvantages of choosing this route, should your customer be unable to pay, are:

- the cost of winding-up can be substantial
- these costs may not be fully recoverable
- your customer has secured creditors, whose claim will have priority over yours
- your debt will be among a long list of unsecured creditors.

Whilst statutory demands can be effective in collecting a debt, they should not be abused. Once you have issued a statutory demand you must follow it through. You must be prepared to make your customer bankrupt, if a sole trader or partnership, or place them into liquidation or receivership if a limited company.

ISSUING A STATUTORY DEMAND

The forms required to issue a statutory demand are form 4.1 for an individual or partnership, form 6.1 for a limited company. These can be obtained at any good law stationers, together with form E1 and F1 referred to in Chapter 8. A solicitor is not required to complete or serve these demands: you can very easily do it yourself.

Completing a statutory demand
Even if you are using this method of collection as a bluff, it is advisable to be aware of the procedure. Being able to quote the relevant Acts when talking to your slow paying customers will impress them. They will think you have undertaken this route successfully many times, and hopefully pay up promptly.

Forms 6.1 and 4.1
These two forms carry sufficient instructions to allow you to complete them without requesting legal assistance. They clearly tell the debtors what they must do, and the consequences of ignoring the demand.

Both forms are practically identical and will ask you to state:

Page 1
- the defendant's name and address
- your name and address
- amount of the debt.

Page 2
- particulars of the debt
- when the debt was incurred
- the amount due at the date of the demand.

Page 3
- name and address of the county court the petition was made
- name and address of any other interested party, for communication of the demand
- notes on how to comply with the demand.

Issuing a statutory demand on a limited company
Your pre-sue search will tell you where your debtor's registered office is situated: it is here and not their head office that the demand must be served. It should be accompanied by a simple letter stating that you are enclosing the demand. If practical it is also helpful to fax a copy of the letter and statutory demand to your debtor. This will ensure the whole office staff will see it, embarrassing the management into paying up promptly.

Issuing a statutory demand against an individual or partnership
Again the services of the courts or a solicitor are not required. However, the form must be personally served on the debtor, or debtors if a partnership. You can serve it yourself or use a process server or a certified bailiff. If you do it yourself, you must, before handing over the envelope containing the statutory demand, confirm that the recipient is indeed the person named on the demand. It cannot be served through a third party.

What you must do after serving the demand
It is vital that you make a note of the time, place and circumstances of service. The reason for this is that, after the time has elapsed in which your debtor must respond, you will be required in the case of an individual to swear an affidavit of service. The notes you made at the time of service will be of paramount importance when swearing the affidavit.

A word of caution
When serving a statutory demand on a limited company, the code of service states it should be left at the registered office of the company: some courts now require an affidavit of service to be sworn. This must show good reasons for believing the demand was brought to the attention of a director. Therefore it is advisable when handing the statutory demand to an employee of the company that you ask them to hand it to a named director or senior manager of the company. Ask the person to whom you hand the demand for their name and position in the company and make a note of the details for your affidavit of service. If possible fax a copy of the affidavit and the accompanying letter, for maximum effect.

What your debtor can do on receipt of a statutory demand
It does not matter if your debtor is a limited company, a partnership or an individual. They must, after receiving a statutory demand and within the time scale allowed, either:

- ignore it, and hope you are bluffing

- pay the amount demanded

- submit an offer to pay by instalments

- make an application to have the statutory demand set aside.

Using the statutory demand can speed the process of payment. But this method of collection must be used with diligence. If you use it as a bluff, you could score an 'own goal'. Use it too often and you are liable to lose all credibility with your customers: it will eventually have the same effect as sending them a monthly statement, and the last thing you want is to be kept waiting for the money due to you.

UNDERSTANDING BANKRUPTCY, RECEIVERSHIP AND LIQUIDATIONS

The purpose of this section is not to encourage you to use these methods to enforce payment – they are generally not cost effective methods to use where an unsecured trade debt is involved. But there will be occasions, no matter how careful you have been in monitoring your customers' creditworthiness, when you will be faced with an insolvency situation. When this unpleasant event does take place, you should be familiar with the procedures you can encounter.

Bankruptcy

Bankruptcy relates only to partnerships and to individuals. A bankruptcy petition is merely a function to stop a person or a number of people from handling their financial affairs, except through a third party. It is used when someone is deemed incompetent to manage their own monetary business. Once a statutory demand has been served on an individual, the routine is similar to that used for a limited company.

Liquidations

These relate to companies which offer their shareholders, the owners, limited liability. Normally you become aware that a customer is insolvent only when their payments become erratic and then cease. The next thing to happen is you receive notice of a 'creditors' meeting' accompanied by a proxy form. This meeting, which has been called under section 98 of the Insolvency Act 1986, is commonly referred to as a 'creditors' voluntary liquidation'. This notice will tell you the time and place of the meeting of the company's creditors.

Form of proxy

It is essential you complete and return the form of proxy together with the fullest details and proof of your debt. This ensures that your debt is registered and will be included in any payout, if sufficient funds are available after the secured creditors have been paid. A copy invoice and/or rental or lease agreement are ample proof of a debt. It is not essential for you to attend. You will be sent details of the meeting at a later stage.

Receivership

Receiverships occur when a secured creditor, usually a bank, appoints an insolvency practitioner to look after its interests. The bank will probably have a fixed and floating charge over the company's assets. In these circumstances the receiver's main task is to evaluate the company's assets and dispose of sufficient of those to settle the bank's debt. Any balance of cash is handed back to the company. The receiver will have no powers to deal with the claims of any unsecured creditors, which are most trade debts such as yours. But he or she will ask all creditors for details of their debts, as this will assist him or her to ascertain the full depth of the company's deficiency. Although the receiver's primary duty is not to the unsecured creditors, he or she must within three months of appointment call a meeting of all creditors to report in full on the progress made.

VOLUNTARY ARRANGEMENTS

There could be occasions when you are involved in a voluntary arrangement. A business will consult an insolvency practitioner when they cannot meet their obligations. They believe their financial difficulties are only temporary, and with strong management guidance and budgetary control the business can be returned to profitability or sold. A voluntary arrangement stops a creditor suing a debtor or putting a company into liquidation. The insolvency practitioner's first task will be to draw up a business plan and proposal document. This will list all the assets and liabilities of your debtor alongside firm details of how they intend to pay all creditors.

ADMINISTRATION ORDERS

Administration orders are voluntary arrangements which can be used by a qualifying debtor: an individual who has more than one creditor and finds themselves unable to meet all their financial obligations. To qualify for an administration order the debtor must have:

- two or more outstanding debts
- at least one must be a high or county court judgement
- total debts of not more than £5,000.

Reasons for requesting an administration order
An administration order allows the debtor to make one affordable payment to the court, at agreed intervals. This is then distributed proportionately among the creditors of the debtor.

Better chance of recovery
As a creditor you have a better chance of recovering what is owed to you under this arrangement than by forcing a bankruptcy petition. The debtor, by showing a responsible attitude, will usually maintain payments; you will not be required to compete with rival creditors for payment from limited resources (it is the largest ones that always seem to get paid in these circumstances). Although it will take longer to recoup your debt, it is better to be paid little and often than not at all.

QUESTIONS AND ANSWERS

Is a debt for goods supplied a secured or unsecured debt?

Most trade debts of this description are classed as unsecured debts.

How long does a debtor have to reply to a statutory demand?

A limited company has 21 days to reply to a statutory demand. An individual, on the other hand, has only 18 days in which to act.

Is it worth putting a company into liquidation for an unsecured debt?

Generally speaking no. But there are some businesses whose policy it is not to pay any accounts until a summons or statutory demand arrives. The best advice in these cases is not to deal with them except on a COD basis.

What must I do if a debtor ignores a statutory demand?

You must employ a solicitor to commence winding-up procedures, you cannot undertake this yourself. But if a company or individual ignores a winding-up petition your chances of recovering your debt must be considered very slim.

Must I attend a creditors' meeting to get paid?

No. Your proxy form can name someone to attend on your behalf. It also ensures you get paid if funds are available. Most of the large accountancy firms supply reports of creditors' meetings free of charge.

What happens at these meetings?

If you attend you can question the directors about their management of the company. But usually these meetings are dominated by a few secured creditors and there is little point in travelling great distances on these occasions.

CHECKLIST

- It is not necessary to issue a statutory demand via the court.
- A statutory demand must never be served through a third party.
- A note must be made at the time of service, for your affidavit.

- You must complete and return your proxy form before the date of a creditors' meeting.

- Have you faxed a copy of the statutory demand for maximum effect?

CASE STUDIES

Bill serves a statutory demand

Deciding he's not prepared to mess around with issuing a summons, Bill Swift completes the statutory demand form and serves it on his debtor. Wrongly believing his customer would not wish to be wound-up, and he will get the money he is due quickly, Bill takes the statutory demand to his customer's registered office. He asks one of the staff to hand the demand to the managing director and makes a note of her name, date and place of delivery for the affidavit he may need to swear later.

Unfortunately Bill Swift's ploy does not work. Instead of receiving a cheque he receives notice from an insolvency practitioner stating that his customer is entering into a voluntary arrangement with their creditors, thereby freezing Bill's action. Now he cannot do anything until he receives details of the debtor's plans to repay what is owed.

Karen goes to a creditors' meeting

Receiving notes of a creditors' meeting relating to one of her larger customers, Karen completes the form of proxy and sends details of her claim to the liquidator. On the day of the meeting she decides to attend. Arriving at the venue, she discovers most of the people present are either secured creditors or accountants attending on behalf of their larger clients, and bank officials. The liquidator is there with one or two directors of the company, one of whom is chairman of the meeting. (Some people when completing their proxy form tend to nominate as their proxy the chairman of the meeting. Avoid this at all costs, because he will be a director of the company which owes you money.)

Finding the meeting dominated by the secured and larger unsecured creditors, Karen resolves not to waste time attending any other creditors' meetings in future but to deal with them at a distance concentrating her efforts on the debts she can collect.

Ted receives a statutory demand

Receiving a statutory demand from Bill Swift, Ted Knavish feels aggrieved that no one from Bill's firm contacted him to discuss his problem – not realising it was his responsibility to approach Bill Swift. Knowing his financial problems are only temporary, and not wishing to be made bankrupt and lose his business, he calls round to see Bill and explain his current embarrassment. They come to an amicable agreement. If Bill had maintained regular contact with his customer, or if Ted had not ignored his problems, hoping they would go away, an arrangement to settle the outstanding account could have been agreed months ago.

DISCUSSION POINTS

1. What do you think are the advantages of a voluntary arrangement for both creditor and debtor?

2. Can you think of examples in your area of companies going into liquidation or receivership?

11
Civil Law in Scotland

HOW SMALL CLAIMS DIFFER

The underlying principles for making a claim in Scotland are the same as in the rest of the British Isles. Scottish courts offer you the same basic rights for recovering money owing to you and resolving disputes as explained throughout this book.

Where the procedures vary

Variations mainly relate to changes in titles of the court officials, debtor and creditor; these comparisons are to be found in the Glossary. The forms required for issuing a summons also differ from those used earlier, and the kind of summons you can bring fall into distinct formats, although their aims remain the same:

- form 1 – small claims summons for the payment of money

- form 15 – small claims summons for delivery or recovery of possession of moveable property

- form 18 – small claims summons for the implementation of an obligation.

Instead of using the county court, as described earlier, you pursue your claim through the sheriff court. If you reside outside Scotland a full list of sheriff courts are obtainable from the Scottish court service (see Useful Addresses).

Small claims in the sheriff court
The maximum amount you can claim in the sheriff small claims court is restricted to £750. For sums above this figure, you must use the summary cause procedure. This procedure is similar to the county court system described earlier. If you are suing for sums in excess of £750, you should seek advice from the court service or your local:

- Citizens Advice Bureau
- Trading Standards officer
- sheriff's court.

TYPES OF CLAIMS

As stated, there are three main types of claim you can make in the sheriff small claims court. These are subject to the financial limits referred to previously, and are now explained in a little more detail.

Claims for a debt

These refer to the sort of claims we were pursuing in the earlier chapters. A typical claim could result from:

- a trade debt
- money due from a private loan or rent
- damage to property, resulting from a car accident for example.

Other types of claim

Claims other than for the recovery of money due fall into two distinct classifications. Different forms are used for each type of claim, and these claims are as follows:

Delivery or recovery of moveable property

You can issue a summons under this heading if, for example, you sent your television in for repair, and after a reasonable period of time it was not returned and you were not content with the explanation given by the repairer. You could also claim for money for loss of use and inconvenience. You could also use this summons if you were a shop-keeper who sold goods on hire purchase or rental whose customer failed to maintain payments; you could sue for the recovery of the goods, in addition to any arrears due under the terms of the contract.

Claim for implementation of an obligation

An 'implement of an obligation' simply means you require the court to order another person or firm to do something. For example, a tradesman might fail to complete a repair for an appliance under guarantee. The people you sue could be a:

- tradesperson
- repairman

- manufacturer

- garage owner.

STARTING A CLAIM IN THE SHERIFF COURT

You cannot commence an action in your local county or sheriff court unless you live or your business is situated in Scotland. Even so, if the defender lives outside your local court's jurisdiction you must issue the proceedings in their local court.

Claims for money owed

Form 1 is a fairly straightforward form to complete. On the front page only parts 1 to 4, and the statement of claim on the second page, have to be filled in by you. (An example of the first page is shown in Figure 21. The statement of claim on page 2 is the same as the particulars of claim shown in Figure 3.) Pages 3 and 4 of form 1 are for the court's use. To complete the form you must enter in:

Box 1.   The name, address and telephone number of the sheriff court where the summons is to be issued.

Boxes 2   The name and address of the firm or person against and 3.   whom you are making a claim.

Box 4.   The standard parts of the form marked 1 and 2 should be left. In part 3 fill in the amount of your claim. In part 4 insert the amount of interest you are adding to your claim (check with the court for the current rate of interest you are allowed to charge).

Box 5.   Will be completed by the court staff.

Box 6.   Should be left blank unless you intend using a solicitor.

Completing the defender's copy
After you have filled in the summons form, a copy of the summons which will be submitted to the defender must be completed. The two types of copy summons are:

- form 2 for claims against individuals, such as sole traders

- form 3 to be used against companies.

Form 2 allows the defender to make an application for time to pay. Companies are not allowed to request time to pay, thus the reason for a separate form. Examples of these forms can be seen in Figure

Small Claim Summons

Claim for Payment of Money

Sheriff Court (name, address and tel. no.)

1

SHERIFF COURT
LAW ST AYR
01292 379 585

Name and address of person making the claim. (PURSUER)

2

WILLIAM SWIFT
16 OLD TOWN ST
GLASGOW

Name and address of person from whom money is claimed (DEFENDER)

3

EDWARD Mc KNAVISH
NEW TOWN ST
AYR

4

CLAIM
The Pursuer claims from the Defender the sum of £ ___ 475 . 00 ___

with interest on that sum at the rate of **15** % annually from the date of service and expenses.

5

RETURN DATE		19	
PRELIMINARY HEARING DATE		19	at	am

*Sheriff Clerk to delete as appropriate

The pursuer is authorised to serve* form 2/form 3, which is a service copy summons, on the defender not less than 21 days before the RETURN DATE shown in the box above. The summons is warrant for arrestment on the dependence.

Sheriff Clerk Depute .... Date .... 19 .....

Name, full address and tel. no. of pursuer's solicitor (if any)

6

NOTE:

The person making the claim (the pursuer) should complete boxes 1,2,3,4 and 6 on this page and the statement of claim on page 2 and the Sheriff Clerk will complete box 5 when he receives this form from the pursuer.

Fig. 21. Small claims summons, Scotland (form 1).
(Reproduced with permission of HMSO.)

22, for pages 3 and 4 of form 2, and Figure 23 for page 3 of form 3.

Serving the defender's copy
Once the requisite forms have been completed, take them along to your defender's local sheriff court, with the required fees for issue. At the court the sheriff clerk will complete box 5, and he or she will endorse the documents. The defender's copy will be sent to them by recorded delivery. As in the rest of the British Isles, the summons can be served upon the defender by a sheriff's officer for a small additional fee.

What the defender must do
The court staff will have entered onto forms 1 and 2 the date for the preliminary hearing. The defender's options are exactly as described for the rest of the United Kingdom, except that he has up to seven days before the hearing to respond.

Pre-sue routines
Obtaining a pre-sue report, and preparing your case as per the earlier chapters, are equally as important when suing in Scotland.

HOW TO ACT AT A PRELIMINARY HEARING

Procedures in these hearings are similar to those described earlier. Both you as the pursuer and the defender will act and conduct the case as if it were anywhere else in the British Isles. You can:

- object to the court's decision

- agree or disagree with the defender's offer of payment

- make applications; to ask the defender to do something or adjourn proceedings

- call a witness.

If the defender fails to pay
Should payment not be made by the defender as decreed, the whole amount outstanding becomes due and payable if the decree was for timed payments. You can request the court to seize household goods and effects, the defender's wages can be arrested if they are in employment, or you can arrest bank or building society accounts. These methods are explained in Chapters 8 and 9.

YOUR RESPONSE TO THE SUMMONS

CLAIM ADMITTED—Under The Debtors (Scotland) Act 1987

The Act gives you the right to apply to the court for a "time to pay direction" which is an order saying that you can pay any sum you are ordered to pay to the pursuer either in instalments or by deferred lump sum. A deferred lump sum means that you must pay all the amount at one time within a specified period set by the court

In addition when making a "time to pay direction" the court may recall or restrict an arrestment made on your property by the pursuer in connection with the action or debt (for example your bank account may have been frozen)

If the court makes a "time to pay direction" a copy of the court order (called an extract decree) will be served on you by the pursuer telling you when payment should start or when it is you have to pay the lump sum

If the court does not make a "time to pay direction" and makes an order for immediate payment against you, an order to pay (called a charge) may be served on you if you do not pay

---

Box 1

ADMIT THE CLAIM—and make written application to pay by instalments or deferred lump sum

I do not intend to attend court but admit the claim and wish to make a WRITTEN APPLICATION about payment

I have completed the application form in section B on page 4.

Signature ....

Box 2

ADMIT THE CLAIM—INTENTION TO APPEAR

I admit the claim and INTEND TO APPEAR OR BE REPRESENTED IN COURT.

Signature ....

Box 3

DENY THE CLAIM—INTENTION TO APPEAR

I do not admit the claim. I intend to appear or be represented in court to state my defence.

*I intend to challenge the jurisdiction of the court.

*I attach a note of my proposed defence which has been copied to the pursuer.

Signature ....   *Delete as necessary

PLEASE REMEMBER

Send pages 3 and 4 to the court to arrive on or before the return date if you have signed any of the responses above. If you have admitted the claim do not send any payment to the court.

Fig. 22. Debtor's response to the summons, Scotland (pp 3 and 4, form 2).
(Reproduced with permission of HMSO.)

Fig. 22. (continued).

YOUR RESPONSE TO THE SUMMONS

SECTION B
DENY THE CLAIM—INTENTION TO APPEAR

I do not admit the claim I intend to appear or be represented in court to state my defence

*I intend to challenge the jurisdiction of the court
*I attach a note of my proposed defence which has been copied to the pursuer

Signature ....   *Delete as necessary

PLEASE REMEMBER

Send this page to the court to arrive **on or before the return date** if you have signed the above box. If you have admitted the claim do not send any payment to the court.

Fig. 23. Debtor company's response to the summons, Scotland (p3 of form 3). (Reproduced with permission of HMSO.)

130

Recalling a decree

This is the same as making an application to reissue a summons, which was described in Chapter 3. The situations that allow a decree to be recalled are where judgements were awarded in the following circumstances:

- an order was made against a pursuer, because they failed to appear or were not represented at the preliminary hearing

- an order was made against a defender who failed to appear at a hearing

- when a claim for money decree was awarded against a defender, and he or she failed to submit an offer to pay.

Making an application in Scotland

You can make an application to the court for the same reasons as in England and Wales. There are no printed forms for an application. All you need to do is to state your reason for the application in writing, give the details of the case, sign and date the document. A defender may make an application for an order to recover an invoice they do not have in their possession. They would simply state the details as outlined in Figure 24.

Sheriff Court: Ayr

Summons No: 123 of 26.10.9X

Date of next hearing: 2 February 199X

William Swift (Pursuer) v Edward McKnavish (Defender)

The defender seeks an order for the recovery of copy invoices number 1 & 2. These documents are held by the pursuer, at his place of business, 1 Old Town Street, Any Town.

Date: 4th November 199X _____DEFENDER

Fig. 24. Making an application in Scotland.

QUESTIONS AND ANSWERS

Must I attend court if I live in England?

Yes, unless you want to instruct a solicitor. This is one of the disadvantages if you trade across the border.

Have you explained all the procedures in Scotland?

No. The idea of this chapter is to give you a broad understanding of Scottish litigation. To explain all the systems of summary cause procedure and enforcement means repeating most of the previous chapters.

Where can I get more information?

The court service in Scotland will supply all the required forms and latest literature, and will help and advise as you proceed. They cannot answer legal questions, however.

Are the forms for obtaining a decree also different?

Yes. The essential pages of the important ones have been illustrated. But help is at hand, see the Further Reading section.

Are all actions commenced in the defender's local court?

Yes. So if your business was in Glasgow, for example, and the defender lived in Ayr, you must start proceedings in the Ayr sheriff court.

Where can I get the addresses of the sheriff courts in Scotland?

From the Scottish court service or your local Citizens Advice Bureau.

Can I claim expenses?

Yes and no. Costs can only be added when the amount of your claim is between £200 and the £750 limit. The amount of costs you can claim is restricted to a maximum of £75. Unlike England and Wales no awards for expenses are made for judgements under £200. Any expenses which are awarded only apply to defended cases.

CHECKLIST

You are claiming for money against a customer in Scotland. Have you:

- completed pre-sue procedures
- checked the location of the defender's local court
- filled in forms 1 and 3
- sent them to the court with copies of your evidence *ie* invoices
- noted the date of the preliminary hearing in your diary
- prepared your case thoroughly?

CASE STUDIES

Bill is put off issuing a summons in Scotland

After applying for information from the sheriff court in the area where his customer lives, he decides the cost of travelling to Scotland for a small claim is prohibitive. He places the debt with a reputable firm of debt collecting agents who have offices in Scotland, and sits back to await results.

Karen takes a chance

The court service in Scotland sends Karen an information pack and a supply of forms. She found the staff when she telephoned very helpful and friendly. Realising the procedures were not unlike the ones she now uses quite confidently in England, she issues a summons. Her debtor, a sole trader, admits her claim and requests a time payment decree. Accepting their offer, she finds that the debt is repaid over a reasonable period of time.

Ted gets a summons from a Scottish supplier

The differing routines which operate in Scotland do not affect Ted Knavish, as the pursuer must issue the summons in England, and conduct the action under the system used in England and Wales. Were the pursuer permitted to commence their action in Scotland, Ted Knavish could make an application to have the action transferred to his local court.

DISCUSSION POINTS

1. What type of small claim is most likely to be of relevance to you?

2. If you live outside Scotland, what level of claim do you think would be worth pursuing across the border?

Glossary

Absolvitor. (Scot.) An order which rules out any further action against the defender.

Admissible. Usually referring to any evidence which can be used in a court of law.

Admission. The agreement by the other party to your stated claim.

Advocate. (Scot.) A barrister, a person who pleads or argues on behalf of another.

Appeal. A request to the court to reconsider its decision.

Appellant. (Scot.) Anyone who appeals against a court's decision.

Applicant. (N.I.) The person or firm who makes an application in the province.

Application. A formal request to a court for either the court or the other party to the action to do something.

Application for arbitration. (N.I.) The procedure used for commencing a small claim in the province.

Arbiter. A judge or someone in authority who has control over a hearing or arbitration.

Arbitration. The method of settling a dispute or claims for money by mutual agreement, either by a court or non-court negotiator.

Arbitrator. A person appointed to settle a dispute or a claim for money.

Arrestment. (Scot.) An order seizing wages or money held in banks or building societies by decree of the sheriff court to settle a judgement order.

Arrestment on the dependence. (Scot.) An order to freeze goods belonging to the defender until the case has been heard.

Asking for leave. A request to the court seeking permission to do something, for example to introduce new evidence not previously disclosed.

Attachment. Legal seizure of assets, usually associated with earnings.

Bailiff. A court officer who is empowered to execute writs and warrants, and process and carry out distraints and arrests.

Bailiwick. The district or jurisdiction of a bailiff.

Barrister. A person called to the bar who is entitled to practise in the higher court.

Bench. The judge's seat in court, the office of a judge or magistrate, and a division of the high court.

Case number. The reference or file number of your summons, sometimes referred to as a plaint number. This number must be quoted in all correspondence to the court.

Certificate. (Scot.) The declaration on the court forms which you must sign confirming the amount of judgement remaining unpaid contrary to the order or decree.

Chambers. The judge's private room where informal hearings are held.

Charging order. An order or decree preventing the defendant from selling his house or land unless you are paid what is owed.

Citation of defender. (Scot.) The notice on the defender's copy summons which must be signed by the court official sending the copy summons to the defender.

Civil actions. Lawsuits which restrict themselves to non-criminal matters.

Claim. A demand for one's dues. The request or order for the repayment of money, or return of goods.

Claimant. The person who is making a claim in a lawsuit.

Clerk of the court. A senior officer in charge of the court's administration.

Continuance. An order or decree made by a judge continuing the case over to another day or time for a specific reason.

Costs. An award for reclaiming the expenses involved for issuing a summons or warrant.

County courts. A judicial court for hearing civil actions for the recovery of money due or to settle disputes.

Creditor. A person or firm to whom a debt is owed.

Debtor. Some person or business who owes a sum of money to a creditor.

Decree. (Scot.) A judgement order or award in the sheriff court.

Defence. The argument put forward by a defendant or defender disagreeing with your claim against them.

Defendant. The person or firm against whom a summons is issued.

Defender. (Scot.) A person or firm against which a claim is made in the sheriff court.

Dismissal. An order bringing an end to the proceedings or the case, for example due to lack of evidence.

Directions. Instructions from the court telling you what you must do, or what evidence you should bring along to the court.

Disclosure. The act of revealing evidence, or advising the court and the other party you intend to call as a witness.

Disposal hearing. A hearing, usually in chambers, when either the plaintiff or defendant disagrees with the court's decision. The aim of the hearing is to discover the point of disagreement, while determining what other evidence or witnesses are required, and the length of time the case will take to be heard.

Distraint. An order in law for the seizure of goods and chattels to make a person pay a debt or meet an obligation.

District judge. A public officer appointed to hear and try cases in both the county and small claims courts.

Evidence. The facts and statements given orally or in writing in the court supporting your argument or claim.

Execution of service. The act of sending the notice of proceedings to the defendant, or to carry out an order of the court.

Full hearing. A hearing which is conducted in an open court.

High court. The senior of the civil courts which hears cases not suitable for the county or small claims courts, such as action which could set legal precedents or where the claim is in excess of £25,000.

Incidental applications. (Scot.) An application which is made during the course of a small claim for an order requesting the other party to do something.

Jurisdiction. The authority of the court to hear certain cases.

Lay representative. Someone other than a solicitor called to speak on behalf of a plaintiff or defendant.

Notification. (N.I.) A notice from the county court to the applicant and responder which states the amount of judgement and costs awarded.

Ombudsman. An official appointed to investigate individual complaints made against public authorities, financial, and legal institutions.

Out of court settlement. Agreement reached prior to a hearing by both parties of the claim or dispute to reach a settlement or pay a debt.

Parties to the action. All the people involved in a lawsuit, such as defendants, plaintiffs and witnesses.

Plaintiff. A person or firm bringing a court action against a debtor for the recovery of money owed, or one wishing to settle a dispute.

Pleadings. Court forms, formal statements and arguments.

Preliminary hearing. The first time a claim or dispute is heard in a court; the hearing can either conclude an action or decide on the best methods of procedure.

Pursuer. (Scot.) The person or business making a claim in the sheriff court.

Recall of a decree. (Scot.) A procedure for changing the decision of the sheriff court when either the pursuer or defender in a claim failed to attend a court hearing.

Recovery of documents. An order allowing the other party to make available evidence which is not in the possession of the person seeking it.

Regulator. An official appointed to monitor and investigate complaints made against public utilities.

Respondent. (Scot. and N.I.) The person or business against whom a claim or complaint is made in Northern Ireland. In Scotland it is the party to the action who is not appealing against a court's decision.

Service. The delivery of a writ, warrant or other court documents either by post or by a court official upon one party on behalf of the other in a legal action.

Sheriff. (Scot.) A person appointed judge, who will hear your claim or dispute and arrive at a decision.

Sheriff court. (Scot.) The Scottish equivalent to a county or small claims court.

Sheriff's officer. (Scot.) A Scottish bailiff, one who carries out distraints and arrests.

Small claims court. The section of the lower courts which deals with all claims under £3,000 in England and Wales, £1,000 in Northern Ireland and £750 in Scotland.

Solicitor. A qualified member of the legal profession, who advises clients on matters of law, and who can instruct barristers.

Summons. The principal court document, containing the full details of a claim or dispute, used to commence a legal action.

Time to pay. A request or order allowing a defendant to pay the judgement debt or decree in a monetary claim by instalments.

Usher. An official of the court who assists the judge and organises the hearings.

Warrant. A written authorisation from the courts allowing for something to be done or goods and chattels to be seized.

Witness. Someone who attests confirmation of your statement, condition of goods; an expert who gives evidence.

Useful Addresses

CREDIT REFERENCE AND COLLECTIONS

Commercial Collection Services, 797 London Road, Thornton Heath, Surrey CR7 6YY. Tel: (0181) 665 4900. Fax: (0181) 683 2283.

Dun & Bradstreet Ltd, Holmers Farm Way, High Wycombe, Buckinghamshire HP12 4UL. Tel: (01494) 422 000. Fax: (01494) 422 260.

Trade Indemnity Collections Ltd, 1 Canada Square, London E14 5DX. Tel: (0171) 739 4311. Fax: (0171) 860 2651.

PRIVATE ARBITRATORS

ADR Group, Equity & Law Building, 36-38 Baldwin Street, Bristol BS1 1NR. Tel: (0117) 925 2090. Fax: (0117) 929 4429.

Centre for Dispute Resolution, 100 Fetter Lane, London EC4A 1DD. tel: (0171) 481 4441. Fax: (0171) 430 1846.

Chartered Institute of Arbitrators, 24 Angel Gate, City Lane, London EC1V 2RS. Tel: (0171) 837 4483. Fax: (0171) 837 4185.

LEGAL MATTERS

Office of Fair Trading, Field House, 15-25 Breams Buildings, Fetter Lane, London EC4A 1PR. Tel: (0171) 242 2858. Advice and information on all matters relating to consumer finance.

The Court Service

England & Wales: Southside, 105 Victoria Street, London SW1E 6QT. Tel: (0171) 210 1708. Fax: (0171) 210 1679.

Northern Ireland: Windsor House, 9-15 Bedford Street, Belfast BT2 7LT. Tel: (0232) 328 594. Fax: (0232) 439 110.

Scotland: Hayweight House, 23 Lauriston Street, Edinburgh EH3 9DQ. Tel: (0131) 221 6889. Fax: (0131) 221 6890.

The court service will supply you with an address list of county or sheriff court offices in the area of their jurisdiction. They will also supply you with most forms free of charge to pursue your claim if you live or work outside their district. However, whenever possible your first point of enquiry should always be your local court.

Further Reading

BUSINESS MATTERS

Credit Management Handbook, H Edwards (Gower, 1990).
How to Get Debts Paid Faster, Roy Hedges (Gower, 1989).
Managing Budgets & Cash Flows, Peter Taylor (How To Books, 2nd edition, 1996).
Managing Credit, Roy Hedges (How To Books, 1997).

GENERAL

The Indebted Society – Credit and Defaults, Janet Ford (Routledge, 1988).

LEGAL

A Guide to Small Claims in the Sheriff Court (HMSO).
New Procedures for Debt Collection in Scotland (HMSO).

Index